MENTAL
HEALTH
and
SOCIAL
POLICY

PRENTICE-HALL SERIES IN SOCIAL POLICY

Howard E. Freeman, Editor

David Mechanic

MENTAL HEALTH and SOCIAL POLICY

prentice-hall, inc.,
englewood cliffs, new jersey

Library of Congress Catalog Card No.: 70-81314
Current printing (last digit)
10 9 8 7 6 5 4 3 2 1
Printed in the United States of America

*Prentice-Hall International, Inc., London
Prentice-Hall of Australia, Pty. Ltd., Sydney
Prentice-Hall of Canada, Ltd., Toronto
Prentice-Hall of India Private Limited, New Delhi
Prentice-Hall of Japan, Inc., Tokyo*

TO GLADYS

PREFACE

Mental health is a major American industry. In one way or another, mental health programs are being developed by a wide range of government agencies, private voluntary groups, schools and universities, commercial and industrial enterprises, and even religious organizations. The federal government invests vast resources in mental health care, research, and education; the annual budget of the National Institute of Mental Health alone is approaching 400 million dollars. Such agencies as the National Institutes of Health, the National Institute of Mental Health, the Department of Health, Education and Welfare, the Office of Economic Opportunity, and the Armed Forces have initiated and developed a great variety of demonstration programs, research efforts, and construction plans. From a quick survey of programs and involvements it clearly appears that mental health is everybody's business.

The need for mental health efforts and programs must be measured not only in terms of monetary expenditures but also with regard to the suffering and disability that characterize mental illness. These problems extend well beyond the mentally ill themselves, affecting families, work relationships, and community life in general. The consequences of mental illness are prevalent in almost every area of life, as evidenced by the continuing failure of a large proportion of American young men to meet "mental standards" for service in the Armed Forces.

It is inevitable that such far-reaching problems should be of concern to legislative and executive agencies of the government. Public agencies have traditionally taken some responsibility in the prevention and treatment of mental illness, and as resources available to such agencies increase so does their role in these areas. A coherent public policy is a necessity, not only to meet bureaucratic requirements but also, and more importantly, to use the limited resources available to achieve the best balance of short-term and long-range objectives. A coherent mental health policy requires decisions among various alternatives which depend in part on the definition and resolution of various issues. Much planning in the area of mental health takes place in a context of great uncertainty, which results from a lack of information and understanding in many areas central to decision making. The unknowns in the mental health field force us to make certain assumptions which are, to some extent, arbitrary and not based on a clear body of facts. Whatever the present state of scientific knowledge, it is essential that we at least recognize the issues relevant to public policy decisions, define the alternatives open to us, and consider the probable advantages and disadvantages of each form of action.

It is not my intention to arrive at sweeping general recommendations. Rather, my discussion is an attempt to define the major issues and questions that the mental health planner, practitioner, and research investigator must face, to examine the ambiguities surrounding these issues and the difficulties of resolving them, and to explore some of the investigations and analyses that help clarify them. Although I do put forth some suggestions for mental health policy, my main task is to examine the existing situation in the United States and the choices we face now and may face in the future. Through such an approach, we can better understand the difficulties of developing a coherent mental health policy and more effectively formulate alternatives for the future.

The issues raised in this monograph are a product, in part, of a more specific concern in exploring the utility and implications of using an educational perspective in providing mental health care. As part of a project (R11 MH-02014) supported by the National Institute of Mental Health and concerned with the personal and environmental factors conducive to a higher level of functioning among mental patients, it was necessary to consider the consequences following the selection of one rehabilitation alternative over another. Since few available books raise issues relating behavioral science theory and research to public policy in the mental health field, I welcomed the invitation from the editor of the Prentice-Hall series on the application of the social sciences to put these thoughts together in a book available to students and other interested persons. In writing this book, I have benefited from many discussions with colleagues, not only in my own field but also in psychiatry and law. I wish to thank those of my colleagues who read an earlier draft of the manuscript and made various suggestions for its revision, including Howard Freeman, John Wing, Lee Robins, George Brown, Elmer Gardner, Jack Zusman, and William Bolman. Alexander Brooks and Marygold Melli were very helpful in giving particular attention to Chapter VIII, which concerns their professional specialty. I am also indebted to Manon Spitzer, who provided excellent library assistance and who was tenacious in pursuing particular and elusive historical events, and to Lorraine Borsuk, who typed the manuscript.

DAVID MECHANIC
University of Wisconsin

CONTENTS

MENTAL
HEALTH
and
SOCIAL
POLICY

Chapter 1

MENTAL HEALTH AND THE MENTAL HEALTH PROFESSIONS

Human feelings and behavior are extremely variable. The same person may be happy or sad, energetic or lethargic, anxious or calm depending on his environment and personal life at the time. Many emotions and reactions fall within the normal range since everyday events evoke varying responses from us. To be sad when a loved one dies or to be anxious about an important but difficult examination is a normal response since such a feeling fits the situation. Feelings of sadness, depression, or anxiety in themselves do not constitute abnormal responses unless they are dissonant with social and personal circumstances.

We usually recognize deviations from "normal" mental health in two ways. A person sometimes engages in behavior which is strikingly discordant with his social circumstances and life situation; his behavior or expressed feeling state at such a time is so bizarre and difficult to make sense of that we infer illness. The context of behavior, it should be emphasized, is critical in making most such assessments. Although a person from a cultural background characterized by an organized belief system based on witchcraft might understandably be suspicious and fearful of being poisoned or harmed by magic, a similar reaction by a person born and raised in Akron, Ohio, might leave us puzzled and concerned. When such incongruities develop, they raise issues of mental illness.

Another major way of identifying deviations from mental health is through recognition of personal suffering not easily explained by the life circumstances of the person showing such reactions. Although it may be normal for an unemployed man who cannot adequately provide for his children and who is objectively deprived and discriminated against to feel frustrated and angry, we infer that a person showing a similar reaction under favorable life circumstances and in the absence of any provocation is psychiatrically disordered.

Very bizarre behavior or profound suffering is not difficult to recognize. But much of our social behavior and most of our life circumstances are not so clear cut, and it is not always easy to ascertain whether a particular pattern of behavior or of feelings is inappropriate to or discordant with the social circumstances. Since extensive subgroup differences in value orientations and behavior characterize community life, it is often impossible to decide whether a person's behavior is bizarre or whether he is responding to a set of values characteristic of some subgroup rather than to the dominant or supposedly dominant cultural norm. Hippies may appear bizarre to older and more conventional persons, but their patterns of dress and action are not necessarily discordant with the social scene. Similarly, many aspects of a person's life and personal relationships lead to sadness or anxiety, but they are not clearly apparent unless we explore in some detail that person's real life situation, which may be different from the way it appears.

Attempts to define mental illness in some precise fashion have brought continuing disappointment. Although it is usually defined in terms of some deviation from normality, defining normality is not a simple matter. From a practical standpoint the person himself often becomes aware that something is not quite right and that his feelings, outlook, or state of mind is unusual or aberrant compared with his previous experience or those of other persons. On other occasions, persons other than the one affected come to define his behavior as bizarre because it appears to be inconsistent with usual standards of normality or departs from the ordinary in a manner difficult to understand in terms of what they have learned to expect from him or persons like him. Because the early definition of mental illness depends on lay judgments involving varying criteria, a wide range of behavior patterns are defined as mental illness, and behavior patterns and life problems overlap considerably among those who are defined as ill and those who are not.

All of us, of course, may sometimes digress from usual standards of behavior and expression in a manner which appears strange to others, but these digressions do not lead to a diagnosis of mental illness. Such a diagnosis is ordinarily not considered unless the behavior is persistent or is so bizarre and destructive as to be unexplainable in any other terms. Although mental illness is identified by aberrant acts and expression, the definition extends beyond these acts to implicate the person's entire identity and personality. Thus, when we define such behavior we say not only that the person is behaving in a manner discordant with his circumstances, but also that he is mentally ill or that his mind is disordered. This inference that the person suffers from some condition that permeates his whole being rather than from a more specific defect in learning or interpersonal relations has many consequences which we shall discuss later.

From the perspective of those holding certain values, the definition of mental illness in terms of failures in social adjustment or of deviant response is inappropriate. Some psychologists have argued, for example, that neurotic persons who struggle psychologically and socially against the patterns of their society and who as a result may appear to be misfits in one way or another are more healthy than those who conform easily to all the mandates of their community (Fromm, 1955). In this view, a person who conforms to a sick society rather than struggles against it, such as the mass of the German population who obeyed Nazi mandates, cannot be said to have a high level of mental health. In trying to describe the characteristics of people with positive mental health, some clinicians and investigators have sought to define various persistent aspects of social character or personality which could be viewed independently of the social context. They emphasize such themes as social sensitivity, the capacity for environmental mastery, a unifying outlook on life, self-actualization, and self-acceptance (Jahoda, 1958). However, such themes do not help us identify in any specific way patterns of behavior or feelings which indicate health. Social values and social expectations determine who is socially sensitive or who is achieving self-actualization, and the application of varying sets of values leads to different assessments. Although the concept of positive mental health is one worth keeping in mind, it is not very helpful in classifying different persons, groups, or populations.

Mental health professionals have specific conceptions of mental health and mental disorder; we shall describe these in some detail in Chapter 2. At this point, however, we must define a variety of concepts frequently used in a confusing manner in the mental health field.

Symptoms, Diseases, and Reaction Patterns

Those in the mental health field sometimes do not distinguish between symptoms and conditions. A symptom is a specific deviation from normality, such as high fever, lower-back pain, or apathy and depression. In contrast, a condition is a constellation of symptoms believed to be typical of a particular underlying disorder. Such symptoms as fever, depression, apathy, and loss of appetite may be characteristic of a variety of different conditions; thus information on a particular symptom is usually inadequate for specifying the condition believed to be responsible for it. At times the same word is used to refer to both the symptom and the condition. Thus, the word *depression* describes a particular feeling state on the one hand and a general psychiatric condition on the other. Psychiatrists thus often find themselves in verbal binds, as when they maintain that a patient who is not depressed is suffering from a depressive condition.

The concept of disease is an abstraction. The physician observes certain conditions which appear to fit a particular pattern. He identifies this pattern with a disease label, which often serves as a theory and an explanation of the basic condition troubling the patient. We shall explore the diagnostic process further in the next chapter; we note here, however, that, while some psychiatrists think the observable condition suggests a particular underlying disease, others regard it as nothing more than a typical reaction pattern. The term *reaction pattern* suggests that, although certain symptoms go together, they need not imply any particular disorder. Those who view the behavior of psychiatric patients mostly in terms of reaction patterns in contrast to disease conditions point out that the same condition may manifest itself in many different ways, while different conditions may lead to behavior patterns that are very similar. This view has many roots. Vilfredo Pareto, an Italian sociologist who wrote on this point in the latter part of the nineteenth century, differentiated the deep, persistent, and important aspects of the personality, which he called residues, from the more superficial and varying aspects of the personality, which he referred to as derivations. He maintained that the same residues might lead to widely varying derivations. For example, a love of pornography, a desire to legislate against pornography, and a desire to censor pornography may all be derivations of the same basic residue. Similarly Sigmund Freud, in introducing the concept of reaction formation, posited that a basic human need might find expression through its vigorous denial and repudiation. Much of American psychiatry and clinical psychology is based on the assumption that reaction patterns are not fully meaningful until their psychodynamics have been explored and their basic roots understood. In contrast, European psychiatry places much greater emphasis on the recognition of the basic underlying disease through observation of the patient's symptoms.

Disease, Personality Disturbance, or Problem in Living

Mental health professionals differ considerably in viewing mental illness primarily as a disease, as a disturbance in the functioning of the personality, or as a problem in living. Although these views overlap, emphasis may be put on one perspective or another. Those who view mental illness in disease terms are most likely to believe that constitutional factors are largely responsible for many mental conditions and that genetic and biological factors play an important if not prominent part in explaining the causes of mental illness. Those who view mental illnesses as primarily disturbances of the personality conceive of such problems as repertories of behavior and patterns of feeling which have become deeply rooted as a result of the child's social development and which persist through time, although they are inappropriate to effective social functioning and personal comfort. Finally, some mental health professionals maintain that what is called "mental illness" results in no specific sense from genetic or physical factors or from deep-rooted psychological disorders. They argue rather that such difficulties are problems in living which develop because of confusion in communication, maintenance of particular social rules, and enforcement of certain moral standards. Such theorists maintain that persons are labeled mentally ill because they fail to conform to certain social standards either because of their own unique understandings and viewpoints or because of their failure to develop certain social skills which others define as necessary.

Social Adjustment

In addition to emphasizing bizarre behavior and personal suffering, psychiatrists and other mental health professionals frequently view illness in terms of the failure of persons to adjust adequately to their social surroundings or to fit into a recognized social group. They frequently assume that such adjustment failures result from certain biological or psychological deficiencies in the person. The basic assumption that failure to conform implies disorder leads some mental health professionals to regard all deviants as sick, and they attempt to explain such behavior by seeking its psychological or biological roots. In applying a psychiatric viewpoint to deviance in general, we often fail to appreciate the extent to which nonconforming behavior is a consequence of learning processes whereby persons within particular subgroups and social settings normally develop attitudes, values, and behavior patterns which are illegal or disapproved of within the larger society. No doubt, some deviants suffer from profound psychological disorders, but just as it is irresponsible to argue that all deviant behavior is acquired through normal learning processes, so it is irresponsible and shortsighted to conceive of all behavior we disapprove of as sick.

With so many conflicting views of mental illness, inevitably the conditions so labeled vary widely in character. While some mental health workers view their work as being within a restricted sphere, others feel that they should treat not only patients with problems specifically defined as psychiatric ones but also those who are unhappily married, those who fail to live up to their potential in school, those who are bored and dissatisfied with life, criminals and delinquents, homosexuals and prostitutes, and many others. Because of such multiple definitions of the responsibility of the mental health professions and of the range of the problems they should deal with, it is difficult to describe the work of mental health professionals in a clear and unambiguous manner. Having briefly described the definitions applied by mental health professionals, we turn to a short description of the mental health professions themselves.

The Mental Health Professions

Although particular professional groups are specifically organized to treat or care for the mentally ill, the many problems encompassed by this rubric make it inevitable that many if not most of those suffering from psychiatric conditions receive treatment from persons with little or no special training in treating such disorders. It is impossible to make realistic estimates, but it is generally recognized that many persons who suffer from psychiatric problems receive no treatment at all, and many others receive treatment from only a general medical practitioner. Many patients seen by general practitioners have no significant physical disorders but suffer from psychological distress, alcoholism, depression, phobias, and a variety of other conditions usually dealt with by psychiatric personnel (Shepherd *et al.*, 1966). It is not surprising that so many of these problems are brought to general practitioners—they are often the only professional persons with whom patients have close contact. Other patients may be under the care of clergymen or fringe practitioners, such as chiropractors, or may receive assistance only from friends and acquaintances.

The three main professions organized to provide mental health services are psychiatry, clinical psychology, and psychiatric social work. The psychiatrist is an M.D. who has done postgraduate work in the problems of mental illness. The clinical psychologist, in contrast, is not an M.D. but has had several years of graduate work in psychology and often holds a Ph.D. degree. While the psychiatrist is more likely to have had intensive practical experience in handling psychiatric patients from a clinical perspective during his psychiatric residency, the clinical psychologist is likely to be better versed in psychological theory and research, to better understand the scientific bases of assessment and treatment, and to have a more critical awareness of research. The psychiatric social worker usually holds a two-year postgraduate degree from a social-work training program emphasizing psychodynamic factors and casework.

Each of the three major mental health professions, therefore, reflects a different orientation and background, and each has its distinctive strengths and weaknesses. Although, theoretically, psychiatrists, clinical psychologists, and psychiatric social workers are able to work together in a harmonious team in which their distinctive skills complement one another, not infrequently their relationships are characterized by competition and resentment.

This is not the place to review the legal and political relationships among the different mental health professions. We should note, however, that the medical background of the psychiatrist, with its prestige and implications of medical responsibility, has allowed him to maintain a powerful position relative to the other mental health professionals and at times has allowed him to restrict the scope of their work. The other professionals greatly resent this power for they regard themselves as equally qualified if not more expert than the psychiatrist in assessment and treatment. Both social workers and clinical psychologists, however, often treat patients within social agencies and within other contexts which allow them to maintain their professional autonomy.

Until recently all but the most pronounced psychiatric conditions received no special attention from mental health professionals. For persons with wealth suffering from mental disease, care was available from general medical practitioners or from a small number of private institutions. Prior to the nineteenth century poor insane persons were ignored; if they made a nuisance of themselves they were treated as criminals, and their incarceration was usually degrading and inhuman. With changing conditions in America in the nineteenth century and decreasing tolerance for the mentally ill under the modified social circumstances accompanying industrialization, reform movements developed which advocated building special institutions to separate the mentally ill from criminals and to expose them to a sympathetic environment. In the second part of the nineteenth and early part of the twentieth centuries the number of such institutions increased throughout the United States, but they were largely custodial in character and very inadequately staffed. Although many of these hospitals had psychiatric administrators, American psychiatry did not take root in the hospital context, and consequently these institutions have been traditionally dominated by untrained orderlies.

While psychiatry in Europe developed within the mental hospital system and European psychiatrists contributed to the reform of many of the harsh conditions in these hospitals, American psychiatry went a somewhat different route. American intellectuals were very receptive to the theories and perspectives of Freud; and because of conditions in Europe in the 1930s and particularly the rise of Hitler, many European psychiatrists and Freudian-trained therapists emigrated to the United States and settled in the major intellectual and medical centers. This group of very talented and enthusiastic advocates of psychoanalytic ideas had a profound effect on American intellectual life and thought, which had already begun to show receptivity to the work of Freud. So many of these men came to occupy strategic posts in the centers of psychiatric training in America that psychodynamic views still dominate over other perspectives in the training of American psychiatrists.

Psychodynamic theory had a pervasive influence on the structure of psychiatric care in the United States. The cardinal principle of this perspective is that behavior is dominated by unconscious processes which can contribute to inappropriate social functioning and psychological distress. Only by repeated and intensive exploration between therapist and patient using the psychoanalytic method can these basic unconscious processes be discovered and remedied. Thus, the form of treatment advocated was one expensive in terms of the therapist's time, and since any single therapist could care for only a very small number of patients, it was expensive in terms of money. In short, psychoanalytic therapy required private practice and rich patients. Nevertheless it soon became the dominant activity of American psychiatrists. Henry Davidson (1967), superintendent of Essex County Hospital in New Jersey and editor of *Mental Hygiene,* describes the situation:

> Physicians who want to become psychiatrists now stand at the branching of two roads: one leads to the public hospital, one to the greener backed pastures of private practice. In American public mental hospitals, the 600,000 patients have 3,000 doctors, an average ratio of 200 patients per psychiatrist. The other road as the aspirant sees it, would place him in an office, listening to articulate (and prosperous) young patients (old ones are not wanted). The doctor could practice in this way, content in the knowledge that a "difficult" patient could always be abandoned as poorly motivated; a violent or seriously psychotic one could be dismissed as too sick for outpatient care. He could at a gentlemanly pace, see only a small number of patients, work intensively with their problems, never leave his office to make house calls, testify in court, handle hospital emergencies or otherwise become involved in the labor and drudgery that is the lot of other physicians. Faced with these alternatives, most American physicians (if free to do so) will elect the second image. Thus, the prestigious training programs in the U.S.A. are now the analytically oriented ones. (pp. 340–41)

American psychiatry, thus, has developed differently from psychiatry in other countries. Major cities in America have sufficient persons of means who are intellectually attracted to psychoanalysis and who are willing to pay for it. Since an ample market exists, psychiatrists are trained to meet this demand, and the dominant pattern is for newly trained psychiatrists to seek a private practice. Psychodynamic ideas also have a profound influence on the training of clinical psychologists and psychiatric social workers. Psychodynamic therapy is very much oriented to persons with small or moderate difficulties. Since the development of this therapy stressed verbal and other middle-class abilities and was oriented to treating the neuroses, it was provided largely to educated persons; the poor and those with the most serious and incapacitating conditions had, until the development of psychiatric outpatient clinics, no significant source of help other than hospitalization in a mental institution.

However, the mental hospital offered minimal treatment. Largely custodial in character, overcrowded with patients, and poorly staffed, it frequently did not provide even humane living conditions. A sense of hopelessness prevailed, and the conditions of many patients deteriorated. Such patients were then relegated to back wards, where they were largely ignored until death brought relief to their plight.

Much improvement has occurred in mental hospitals, although they still fall far short of what can and should be done. Most impressive have been large improvements in staffing patterns, particularly in the provision of specially trained psychiatric nurses and of more social workers, psychologists, and other trained persons such as occupational and recreational therapists and vocational counselors. Although these hospitals still depend very heavily on psychiatric aides with limited education and training, they are more carefully supervised than in the past; and it is not uncommon for hospitals to have their own intramural training programs for such staff. Better conditions of work and the new look of hospitals have made these jobs less unattractive; and although hard evidence is difficult to muster, it is generally believed that persons of higher quality are attracted to them.

A survey in 1963 estimated that in the United States there were more than 400 long-stay mental hospitals with a population of more than a half million patients. Although 30 per cent were nongovernment institutions, these cared for only 2 per cent of all patients. Most patients, therefore, were being cared for in very large government hospitals. The largest hospitals were operated by state and local governments, and their average size was 2,000 patients. Federal hospitals, such as those run by the Veteran's Administration, were also large, averaging approximately 1,500 patients (U.S. National Center for Health Statistics, 1965). Increasingly, patients are treated through various outpatient clinics. The number is growing rapidly; in 1963 there were almost 1,800 such clinics, and they provided services to almost a half million persons (Clausen, 1966). The new mental health centers are also taking part of the load. Similarly, with the growth of psychiatric hospitalization insurance, the number of patients cared for in general voluntary hospitals has been increasing. Although efforts are being made throughout the country to reduce the size of mental hospitals and to create new facilities—and some progress has been made since 1963—the large government mental hospitals care for most of these with serious psychiatric conditions.

Public mental hospitals continue to be staffed primarily by non-professional aides, who constitute approximately 90 per cent of the total manpower (Clausen, 1966). Nurses make up more than three-fifths of the total of mental health professionals who work in such hospitals. Psychiatrists and social workers each contribute approximately one-eighth of the total group of professionals and less than 3 per cent of the total mental hospital manpower. Other professionals include psychiatric residents and psychologists (U.S. Public Health Service, 1965). In contrast, outpatient clinics are staffed primarily by social workers and psychiatrists and have a smaller number of psychologists and psychiatric residents. Only a very small number of nurses work in them.

Although there were 3,000 psychiatrists in the United States in 1940, over 5,500 in 1950, and almost 9,000 by 1956 (Felix, 1967), since American psychiatry had developed largely around a psychodynamic perspective, little psychiatric manpower was evident in mental hospitals, where the most seriously disturbed patients were being cared for. In 1950, for example, approximately 85 per cent of psychiatric specialists were engaged outside the mental hospital, although such hospitals had approximately 85 per cent of all resident patients in the United States. Similarly, in 1950 only about one-fifth of the trained psychiatric social workers and only a very small number of psychologists and graduate nurses worked in mental hospitals (Perrow, 1965). The situation was not much better by 1956, when only 1,389 psychiatrists, clinical directors, and psychiatric residents were full-time employees in public mental hospitals (Clausen, 1961, p. 146). A survey of the occupational and personal characteristics of American psychiatrists in 1965 showed that private practice remained the dominant activity (U.S. Public Health Service, 1966). Forty per cent of the psychiatrists in the country were engaged in full-time private practice (defined as 35 hours a week or more), and a majority of all psychiatrists reported heavy involvement in private practice. Only 35 per cent of the more than 14,000 psychiatrists surveyed reported that they spent one or more hours per week in mental hospital work.

Although psychiatric practice is increasingly varied in its character, its two major strains are somewhat different. Most psychiatrists in private practice tend to be committed to a psychodynamic form of therapy in which they interact with patients over some period of time, making use of psychological interpretations. A smaller but also important group of psychiatrists practice by giving supportive and directive therapy, with heavy dependence on drugs and relatively frequent use of physical treatments such as electroshock. Although the use of drugs or physical treatments is not unique to this group of practitioners (for example, many psychiatrists in the former group use drug therapy), such techniques constitute a more important aspect of their therapy than do psychological interpretation and nondirective exploration.

Psychiatrists have been developing many new roles. One of the most important is that of the consultant who advises various community agencies on their programs, difficult cases, and problems, and who serves as a supervisor of other mental health professionals. Thus, the psychiatrist may work with social caseworkers in a mental health center, or he may advise psychiatric residents and nurses in a hospital program. Psychiatrists also frequently involve themselves in matters affecting the courts, community agencies, educational institutions, and even industrial concerns.

Having briefly outlined the character of the mental health professions and their orientations, we must retrace our steps and reconsider in more detail the nature of mental illness and health and the different perspectives toward these subjects held by psychiatrists and other mental health workers.

Chapter 2

WHAT ARE MENTAL HEALTH AND MENTAL ILLNESS?

If we are to discuss mental health policy, we must be aware of the scope and limits of our topic. If our goal is to develop policies to deal with the prevention and treatment of mental illness and the facilitation of mental health, then we must clearly outline the dimensions of each of those concepts. Are mental health programs to be limited to persons who come under the care of mental health workers, or are they to extend to those who see no need for psychiatric services and who have not been defined as problems by their communities? Are such programs to be restricted only to persons suffering from clear psychiatric syndromes, or should they include those with ordinary problems such as nervousness, unhappiness, and social and family conflict? Are deviations such as delinquency and criminal behavior part of the mental health problem, or are they more fruitfully dealt with outside the sphere of psychiatry? Are such situations as poverty, discrimination, and unemployment central aspects of the mental health problem, or do they relate more significantly to other fields? Is failure in performance resulting from a low level of education a mental health problem, or is it primarily a problem of education? Each of these questions and many others must be answered before it is possible to consider alternative mental health policies.

Psychiatrists, mental health workers, and the public in general disagree considerably about the appropriate criteria for ascertaining the presence of mental illness. Much of this disagreement stems from a lack of consensus as to how broad or narrow the conception of mental illness should be. While some psychiatrists restrict the definition of mental illness to a limited set of disorders, others include a great variety of problem situations within the psychiatric sphere.

Psychiatric Diagnostic Models

Traditionally, psychiatrists have developed descriptive diagnostic labels which they use in categorizing and dealing with patients. Although most psychiatrists use these designations, they do not agree on their nature, significance, or utility. Some psychiatrists maintain that the labels denote different disease conditions; others maintain that they apply to reaction patterns having manifest similarities and in no way describe disease conditions. The opinions of most psychiatrists probably fall somewhere between these two; they accept some of the diagnostic categories as disease categories, and they view others as convenient ways of grouping reaction patterns.

The American Psychiatric Association divides psychiatric conditions into three major groups: (1) those conditions caused by or associated with impairment of brain tissue (i.e., disorders caused by infection, intoxication, trauma, metabolic disturbances, etc.); (2) mental deficiency; and (3) disorders without clearly defined clinical cause, those not caused by structural change in the brain, and those attributed to psychogenic causes. We will focus our discussion on this third category.

The American Psychiatric Association further divides this category into five subcategories: (1) psychotic disorders; (2) psychophysiologic, autonomic, and visceral disorders; (3) psychoneurotic disorders; (4) personality disorders; and (5) transient situational personality disorders. Although each of these subcategories is quite ambiguous and has limited diagnostic reliability (that is, psychiatrists frequently disagree as to what the condition is), they descriptively depict the gross reaction patterns recognizable among patients.

From the point of view of psychiatric inpatient care, the psychotic conditions and mental disorders of old age are the central problems. Old persons now constitute approximately one-quarter of all first admissions for long-term care in mental hospitals. Although classified by the American Psychiatric Association as suffering from chronic brain disorders, many of these patients are only moderately senile and could live quite adequately in sheltered environments other than mental hospitals. They often require some nursing attention and are very difficult to care for within a small household. Because of the lack of other suitable facilities, such aged persons are often sent to mental hospitals. The assumption that most of the problems of old age are the result of brain disorders is un-proved, and apart from the diagnosis of arteriosclerosis these assumptions are based totally on observations of behavior (Clausen, 1966). Even the influence of arteriosclerosis is unclear since senility and evidence of arteriosclerosis are not always correlated. Although problems of old age are important and require careful attention, we shall emphasize in this monograph psychotic conditions that develop earlier in life.

The psychotic disorders to which we shall give main emphasis are the affective, the paranoid, and the schizophrenic reactions. The affective disorders involve extreme states of depression or mania, although the former is more common. Depression and other psychoses occurring in late adulthood are given a special designation—involutional psychotic reactions—since they are believed to have some relationship to metabolic and endocrine functions. The paranoid reactions are usually character-ized by persecutory or grandiose delusions, without the occurrence of hallucinations. The suspiciousness characteristic of the paranoid occurs commonly in the general population and does not ordinarily lead to treatment. Some persons with paranoid inclinations become sufficiently disordered and disruptive that they require hospitalization. The schizo-phrenic reactions—the most important in terms of public policy and the need for continuing care—account for approximately one-quarter of all first admissions to mental hospitals and one-half of all patients residing in them. Although psychiatrists generally agree that schizophrenic reactions encompass many different conditions, there is little evidence that subtypes can be reliably differentiated, and under ordinary conditions of practice even the gross diagnosis is less than fully adequate in its reliability. Since schizophrenia is one of the most important psychiatric conditions—and the one most studied and written about—we shall illustrate some of the general problems of psychiatric conceptualization using schizophrenia as an example.

Schizophrenia: An Example in
Psychiatric Conceptualization

Psychiatrists usually diagnose schizophrenia on the basis of bizarre behavior characterized by inappropriate verbalizations and distortions of interpersonal perception as evidenced by the presence of delusions and hallucinations. Schizophrenics often withdraw from interpersonal contacts and engage in a rich and unusual fantasy life. In its more extreme mani-festations, schizophrenia is associated with disregard for conventional expectations and with habit deterioration. According to description schizo-phrenia is a set of reactions involving disturbances in reality relationships and concept formation, accompanied by a variety of intellectual, affective, and behavioral disturbances varying in kind and degree. A. McGhie and J. Chapman (1961) note that early schizophrenia often involves disturbances in the processes of attention and perception (including changes in sensory quality and in the perception of speech and movement), changes in motility and bodily awareness, and changes in thinking and affective processes. Patients classified as schizophrenics often give the impression that they are retreating from reality and appear to be suffering from unpredictable disturbances in their streams of thought. Depending on the stage of the condition and the level of personal deterioration, schizophrenia may be easy or difficult to identify, as F. C. Redlich and D. X. Freedman (1966) note.

> The diagnosis of schizophrenia is either very easy or very difficult. The typical cases, and there are very many such, can be recognized by the layman and the beginner; but some cases offer such difficulties that the most qualified experts in the field cannot come to any agreement. Such difficulties can hardly be surprising; there is no clear fundamental definition of schizophrenia and there are marked differences in international psychiatry as to what is meant by the term. In the United States, the concept of schizophrenia is broader than in the rest of the world and includes marginal types. In general, the diagnosis of schizophrenia is made too frequently; we are inclined to believe that the less skilled the psychiatrist, the more often the diagnosis of schizophrenia. As the diagnosis still has a connotation of malignancy and grave implications for patients and their families, it encourages drastic therapies and should be made with great circumspection. It is based entirely upon psychological and rather subjective criteria. All too often the diagnosis is made without specification of state and severity. (pp. 507–8)

Investigators disagree considerably about the causes of schizophrenia, and theories of conditions so labeled range from biologically oriented models to those which posit the roots of schizophrenia in social interaction, particularly in family life. Implicated in such differences of perspective is the question of whether it is valuable to view schizophrenia as a group of diseases or as a group of problems in living. Those who view schizophrenia as a disease are more careful in specifying precise diagnostic criteria, are more restrictive in the use of the diagnostic label, and are more concerned about diagnostic reliability (Wing, 1967). In contrast, those who view schizophrenia as a convenient term for characterizing a particular reaction pattern which has no generic base use the label more loosely and are less concerned with the reliability of the concept since the diagnosis is not seen as the primary factor in decisions concerning the care and treatment of the patients. This difference in point of view is apparent from the statements below.

> *Constitutional resistance* to the main genotype of schizophrenia is determined by a genetic mechanism which is probably non-specific and certainly

multifactorial. . . . For various reasons it does not seem likely, however, that the genetic mechanisms controlling susceptibility and lack of resistance to schizophrenia—that is, the ability to develop a schizophrenic psychosis and the inability to counteract the progression of the disease—are entirely identical with each other. (Kallman, 1956, pp. 96–97)

Social withdrawal, for example, is a characteristic of most forms of chronic schizophrenia, irrespective of social setting, and a biological component (seen at its most extreme in catatonic stupor) must be accepted. (Wing, 1963, p. 635)

Confusion may arise if one does not keep in mind the nature of the concept of schizophrenia. It is not, and should not be treated as, a disease entity of a biochemical or genetic nature, but merely a reaction type which has been selected more or less arbitrarily because of its operational usefulness. (Ødegaard, 1965, p. 296)

In psychoanalytic terms, the schizophrenics represent those who have failed, due to either somatic or psychogenic forces, to evolve the ego integrative processes or strengths necessary to resolve flexibly conflicts between their (id) drives and overdemanding superego attitudes and aspirations. They are thus defective in their capacity to adapt to the social demands confronting them and to their own drives and they thereby lack a harmonious self-concept and ego ideal with clear goals and motivations. Much of their adaptation is made, instead, through partially satisfying regressive or fixated infantile behavior. (Noyes and Kolb, 1963, p. 325)

We suggest that the double bind nature of the family situation of a schizophrenic results in placing the child in a position where if he responds to his mother's simulated affection her anxiety will be aroused and she will punish him . . . to defend herself from closeness with him. Thus the child is blocked off from intimate and secure associations with his mother. However, if he does not make overtures of affection, she will feel that this means that she is not a loving mother and her anxiety will be aroused. Therefore, she will either punish him for withdrawing or make overtures to the child to insist that he demonstrate that he loves her. . . . In either case in a relationship, the most important in his life and the model for all others, he is punished if he indicates love and affection and punished if he does not. . . . This is the basic nature of the double bind relationship between mother and child. (Bateson *et al.,* 1956, p. 258)

When gross rule-breaking is publicly recognized and made an issue, the rule-breaker may be profoundly confused, anxious, and ashamed. In this crisis it seems reasonable to assume that the rule-breaker will be suggestible to the cues that he gets from the reactions of others toward him. . . . The rule-breaker is sensitive to the cues provided by these others and begins to think of himself in terms of the stereotyped role of insanity, which is part of his own role vocabulary also, since he, like those reacting to him, learned it early in childhood. In this situation his behavior may begin to follow the pattern suggested by his own stereotypes and the reactions of others. That is, when a residual rule-breaker organizes his behavior within the framework of mental disorder, and when his organization is validated by others, particularly prestigeful others such as physicians, he is "hooked" and will proceed on a career of chronic deviance. (Scheff, 1966a, p. 88)

Varying Conceptions of Mental Illness

The descriptions above indicate the many conceptions of the nature and cause of schizophrenia; this situation equally applies to most other mental disorders, and it has led to a vigorous discussion of the concept of mental illness. At one extreme stands Thomas Szasz (1960), a professor of psychiatry and a psychoanalyst, who vociferously maintains that mental illness is a myth and that the standards by which patients are defined as sick are psychosocial, ethical, and legal but not medical. Although Szasz's use of myth metaphor does little to stimulate reasonable and rational debate, he does present a point of view that requires serious scrutiny.

Szasz argues that the concept of mental illness results from conditions such as syphilis of the brain in which it is demonstrable that peculiarities in behavior and thought are linked with a brain condition. He argues that, in contrast, most symptoms designated as mental illness are not brain lesions or similar physical indications, but rather deviations in behavior or thinking. Thus Szasz contends that the metaphor of illness is used to characterize problems having no biological basis and that such judgments are based primarily on ethical or psychosocial criteria. He concedes that specific disorders in thinking and behavior result from brain dysfunctions, but he argues that it is more correct to say that some people labeled as mentally ill suffer from disease of the brain rather than to assert that all of those called mentally ill are sick in a medical sense. In Szasz's opinion, the use of the concept of mental illness to characterize both disorders of the brain and deviations in behavior, thinking, and affect due to other causes results in confusion, abuses of psychiatry, and the use of medical terminology to deprive patients of their civil liberties through involuntary hospitalization and other coercive techniques.

Psychiatrists who oppose Szasz's viewpoint—and they appear to be the majority—contend, in contrast, that they diagnose mental illness not only through the recognition of maladaptive and nonconforming behavior but also through the recognition of manifest disturbances of psychological functioning—delusions, confused perceptions, hallucinations, and such disturbed emotional states as extreme anxiety or depression (Lewis, 1953). Further, they believe that these psychopathological criteria are as valid as the pathological criteria used in the diagnosis of physical conditions. The problem which leads to such great controversy is that in the psychiatric area assessments of pathology depend almost exclusively on the clinician's judgment, while in physical medicine more objective investigatory procedures are frequently available in making such assessments.

One of the typical problems in such debates is that the adversaries are really not addressing themselves to the same point. Szasz bases his argument on the observations that frequently psychiatrists define mental illness solely on the basis of social and psychosocial criteria, that psychiatrists often become involved in questions of ethics and in conflicts of interest rather than being concerned with illness per se, and that the psychiatric role is used to deal with social problems and to achieve social goals which are only remotely related to clinical assessments of pathology; he is correct in all these observations. However, he never really adequately addresses himself to the possibility of assessing mental illness on the basis of disturbances in psychological processes, and it is to this question that his critics usually respond.

Szasz assumes that the disease concept should be reserved for observations demonstrable on a physical basis and therefore that psychological phenomena do not appropriately belong within a disease model. In an essay entitled "Personality Disorder Is Disease," David Ausubel (1961) presents four opposing arguments to the Szasz viewpoint. First, symptoms need not necessarily be a physical lesion to be regarded as a manifestation of disease. Consider, for example, the importance of subjective pain in medicine. Second, it is appropriate to regard psychological symptoms as manifestations of disease if they impair the personality and distort behavior. Third, there is no contradiction in regarding psychological symptoms both as manifestations of illness and as problems. Like physical indications, psychological symptoms may or may not threaten the social adjustment of the person. Finally, immoral behavior and mental illness are clearly distinguishable conditions; the issue of culpability is irrelevant in handling behavior disorders.

Disease concepts are pragmatic instruments, and the reasonableness of applying the diagnostic disease concept to psychiatry depends on its potential use. Medical diagnoses are hypotheses based on some underlying theory or set of assumptions. These underlying theories may be of a scientific or a nonscientific nature, and scientific disease theories may vary widely in their degree of confirmation. The usefulness of a diagnostic disease model depends on its level of confirmation, which depends in turn on the reliability of the diagnosis (the amount of agreement among practitioners in assigning the diagnostic label) and its utility in predicting the course of the condition, its etiology, and how it can be treated successfully (Mechanic, 1968).

The disease models that doctors use in ordinary medical practice vary from those (such as pernicious anemia) based on underlying theories that are well confirmed, to those (such as heart disease, diabetes) based on partially confirmed theories, to those (such as multiple sclerosis) based on unconfirmed theories. Most diseases fall somewhere within the partially confirmed designation. In other words, we know a considerable amount about these conditions, but many important questions are still unanswered. With confirmed disease theories, all the necessary information concerning the cause of the condition, what is likely to occur if it is untreated, and what regimen to apply to retard it is available. A correct diagnostic assessment thus leads to correct action. It should be obvious why diagnostic reliability is so important; if the patient has pernicious anemia and the physician diagnoses his condition as tuberculosis, he will be proceeding on incorrect inferences concerning the cause of the problem and the appropriate actions which will remedy it. (For a more complete discussion of this issue, see Mechanic (1968), pp. 90–114.)

From a theoretical standpoint, we do not have to consider psychiatric conditions as being qualitatively different from nonpsychiatric ones, but, on the whole, the underlying theories concerning psychiatric disorders have a lower level of confirmation than do ordinary medical theories. When a physician assigns the label of pernicious anemia to his patient's condition, his understanding of the patient's problem and his treatment procedure follow directly from the diagnosis. In contrast if, as Ø. Ødegaard (1965) maintains, assignment of the label of schizophrenia to a patient's condition does not affect the choice of therapy or his chance of recovery, we can seriously question the advantage of using the disease model.

In psychiatry, the diagnoses made are not entirely unassociated with the treatment process. Although psychiatrists with a psychodynamic perspective tend to apply a similar approach to most conditions which they regard as treatable, a growing tendency is to use very specific treatments for particular disorders. For example, electroshock therapy appears to be more useful for depressive psychoses than for schizophrenia; behavior therapy, a technique based on learning theory, is used more frequently for phobic reactions than for involutional depression; and the psychiatric drugs used in treating a schizophrenic patient are different from those used in treating a depressed or anxious patient. Obviously, the great deal of overlap in treatment techniques for these various conditions reflects the ambiguous and uncertain state of the field, but the overall level of ignorance is not so large as some would imply.

In deciding whether a disease orientation is useful, it is necessary to balance the gains achieved from using such a perspective against its various disadvantages. The adoption of a disease perspective involves certain risks. For example, characterizing a particular problem as a mental disease may lead to greater stigmatization than would some other way of describing the difficulty. Moreover, the implications that the condition is within the individual rather than in his social situation and that it is not subject to his control or that of others may under some circumstances lead to attitudes on his part and on the part of others in the community that are a serious deterrent to rehabilitation. The most serious result of using disease models when they yield little information is the possible encouragement such a model may provide for failing to explore alternatives for rehabilitation outside the disease perspective. Gerald Grob (1966), an intellectual historian who has studied the history of mental hospital care, notes the following problems.

> The continued insistence by psychiatrists that their profession was truly scientific, however, exerted a profound, though negative, influence over the character of the mental hospital. As we have seen, the assumption that mental disease was somatic in nature invariably led to therapeutic nihilism. Moreover, somaticism often precluded alternative approaches, particularly along psychological and other nonsomatic lines. Lacking any visible means of therapy, psychiatrists tended to engage in a vast holding operation by confining mentally ill patients until that distant day when specific cures for specific disease entities would become available. (pp. 356–57)

The major competing view to the disease perspective is one which conceptualizes problems in terms of their psychodynamics. Instead of concerning himself with establishing a disease diagnosis, the psychodynamic psychiatrist attempts to reconstruct a developmental picture of the patient's personality; he believes that such an exploration will provide an understanding of how the disturbed state of the patient has developed and what functions the disturbed behavior has in his adaptation to the environment. A. P. Noyes and L. C. Kolb (1963), in instructing the psychiatrist on the examination of the patient, make the following observation.

> It will be seen that the mental examination should be a clinical study of personality and aims at a comprehensive appraisal of the patient. Such a study must be made by a genetic and dynamic rather than by a cross sectional method. Only by a genetic-dynamic investigation, with its emphasis on developmental sequence, can one ascertain how the individual came to express himself in his particular form of behavior—that of the neurosis, psychosis, or behavior disorder. The examiner does not seek to make a "diagnosis" in terms of some disease entity. (p. 111)

A basic assumption of the psychodynamic psychiatrist is that disturbed behavior is part of the same continuum as normal behavior and is explained by the same theories that govern our understanding of normal personality development and social functioning. If disturbed behavior is a form of adaptation of the personality in response to particular situations and social stresses, then it is logical to study such behavior from the same perspectives and orientations as those from which we study any other kind of behavior.

The psychodynamic psychiatrist does not make a serious attempt to ascertain whether the patient is mentally ill for this is not a meaningful perspective within his frame of reference. He tends to assume the existence of mental illness or personality disturbance by the fact that the patient is suffering and has come for help or by the fact that the patient's social behavior is sufficiently inappropriate to lead others to bring him to the attention of psychiatric facilities. Using a developmental approach, the psychiatrist attempts to ascertain what aspects of the person's past experience have led him to develop the patterns of functioning that have created the present difficulty. Strong inferences in this approach are that the source of the difficulty is within the person himself and his personality development and that the problem can be alleviated or remedied by changing some aspect of his personality.

Since the psychodynamic perspective does not differentiate mental illness from ordinary problems of mental discomfort or social adjustment, psychiatrists of this persuasion tend to accept for treatment people with a wide variety of problems such as marital dissatisfaction, poor adjustment to school, homosexuality, alcoholism, neurosis, and feelings of lack of fulfillment. Although the psychiatrist may be attuned to some extent to the social aspects of some of these problems, he basically proceeds as though they largely result from the personality of the patient rather than his social situation, deprivation and injustice, or other environmental contingencies. Thus this approach is characterized by a very strong bias— that most problems stem from defects in people and their personality development rather than from external difficulties.

As traditional psychodynamic views have become modified, psychiatrists tend to see difficulties and mental discomfort as the complicated outcomes of the interaction between an individual's personality and the nature of his social environment. Thus, they increasingly recognize that persons with similar personality strengths and weaknesses may make successful or unsuccessful adjustments depending on the social circumstances. For example, a person with strong aggressive needs may or may not have problems depending on whether he is in a position of authority or in a subordinate job. Although this perspective takes the social environment into account, psychiatrists still feel that a well-integrated personality can cope with most circumstances and that persons who get into difficulty usually have significant personality weaknesses. The problem with this assumption is that few people are perfect, and so it is easy to blame any difficulties a person may have on weaknesses or deficiencies in his personality. Negro mothers of illegitimate children may very well have a wide variety of personality problems; but the high rate of illegitimacy among Negroes results largely from the structure of Negro family life, which is the consequence of slavery, impoverishment, discrimination, lack of knowledge about and access to the means of birth control, and a welfare system structured to punish members of intact families. To treat this problem and many others as if responsibility resides in the victim rather than in the social structure is to impose a particular set of values which may have little relationship to reality. The psychodynamic theorist argues that a person raised in an impoverished and deprived environment develops a different personality structure from that of a person raised in privileged and affluent circumstances. Since the psychodynamic theorist does not differentiate the processes underlying normal and abnormal behavior, he might view the personalities of individuals raised under some circumstances as being inimical to adequate social adjustment. Although different social conditions lead to the development of different personality traits, the basis for viewing some traits as adaptive and others as maladaptive is not clear. In the end what is viewed as maladaptive may depend on who the judge is and from what perspective he sees the problem. In short, the psychodynamic view depends very heavily on the value judgments of the therapist.

In contrast, those who view failures in adjustment as being purely the result of environmental circumstances approach the field of mental health with a very different bias. A strict environmental perspective fails to explain why, in the same circumstances, most persons manage to adapt while others have great difficulty. Persons vary widely in their skills, training, and personal characteristics, and a simple situation for some to handle may introduce insuperable barriers and difficulties for others. In the long run, the question of whether it is most appropriate to view the field of mental disorder primarily from the perspective of disease, of psychodynamic development, or of environmental causation depends on future research. No argument, regardless of its sophistication and refinement can, at this point, settle the matter. While it is important to keep an open mind about the ultimate value of using disease models in relation to mental disorders, we must also make sure that the assumption that mental disorders are diseases does not undermine the use of other approaches in helping afflicted persons. Whatever the disease character of mental disorders, such conditions tend to be characterized by various aspects that make them socially different from most nonpsychiatric conditions and which present unique problems in their recognition and care. We now turn to a discussion of some of these characteristics.

Social Conceptions of Mental Illness

We usually recognize and define psychiatric problems, as already noted, through the appearance of particular patterns of deviant behavior or deviant feeling states. Sometimes the person comes to view himself as having a psychiatric problem on the basis of his own conception of normal functioning and on the basis of his knowledge and experience. On other occasions people become aware of their problems as psychiatric ones only after others in their milieu point them out as such. Charles Kadushin (1958) cites an example of how such a definition may be formed.

> I think I have had an emotional disturbance for some time, and I finally decided to do something about it. . . . Before my marriage I had a lot of conflict between my mother and myself. . . . My mother visited us . . . about two weeks ago, and she is always complaining that I never confided in her, and why I wasn't happy at home with my husband . . . and I sort of put the blame on her. She would patch things up after each conflict, and a couple of days after her visit I got an eight-page letter which told me off. She said she noticed my unnatural feelings toward my son. That I give more affection to the cat. . . . Several years ago she said that she would take me to a psychiatrist, without my knowing it. . . . Because, she said, that I didn't love my husband. Now, I didn't see it that way. But now I think I need it. I get upset very easily. . . . I'm very emotional. (p. 395)

On other occasions, the individual or those closest to him resist a definition of mental illness; the person is eventually defined as being mentally ill when a crisis develops because of his bizarre and difficult behavior or when he comes into difficulty with community social agencies. The following example illustrates the process.

> Mr. B's wife had become violently distrustful of him, especially in the past 18 months, but the first indication had come nearly five years ago. He recalled: "It was when Sue (the daughter) was about three months old. My wife was jealous if I played with the baby. She resented it." From this time, Mr. B thought of his wife as having "a nasty streak in her that made her act jealous." She was frequently accusatory and he was frequently angry with her, especially when she falsely accused him of running around with other women. Still, she was a good mother to the children and when she flew off the handle, he would go out for a walk to avoid further conflict. He first thought that the problem might be serious when she said that someone had "done something" to the alarm clock to change its shape. She began to restrict the children's play. When a neighbor came to see how Mrs. B was, she ordered her former friend out of the house, waving a butcher knife. Lorraine B moved out of her husband's bed, but frequently kept him awake much of the night while she prowled the house to "protect her papers and books." These events led eventually to medical intervention. (Adapted from Clausen (1961), pp. 128–29)

In short, the recognition of mental illness generally takes place in community contexts; therefore we should understand how the public forms its conceptions of mental illness.

From the point of view of lay definitions, the two most pervasive and influential perspectives on deviation are those based on the health-illness and the goodness-badness dimensions. Each of these perspectives represents one aspect of our conflicting philosophical conceptions concerning deviant behavior. While we predicate our legal system and much of our social life on the assumptions that man is able to control his actions and that he must be held accountable for his responses (or, in other words, that his actions are consciously motivated and willful), the sciences and scientific perspectives have encouraged a contrasting view of man based on the assumption that deviant behavior is the product of a particular developmental history and cannot be viewed seriously as being within the control of the individual. Because both views are important in social life, we tend to pave a middle path between them, often accepting the assumption of man's accountability for his behavior but at the same time arbitrarily recognizing certain exceptions to this assumption.

The view taken of the deviant depends in large part on the frame of reference of the observer and the extent to which the deviant appears to be willing or able to control his responses (Mechanic, 1962a) The evaluator usually judges the act within the context of what he believes to be the actor's motivation. If the actor's behavior appears reasonable and if it appears to enhance his self-interest in some way, then the evaluator is likely to define the deviant response in terms of the goodness-badness dimension. If the behavior appears to be peculiar and at odds with the actor's self-interest or with expectations of how a reasonable person is motivated, the evaluator is more likely to characterize such behavior in terms of the sickness dimension. Most people, for example, find it difficult to understand why a rich woman would steal small items from the five-and-ten-cent store; they are likely to view such a person as being sick rather than as being bad because it is not clear how such acts serve her interests. In contrast, more people would label the same act committed by a working-class person as being bad. The difference in definition lies not only in the act but also in the motivation imputed to the actor.

Most physical illnesses fall within the usual conceptions of sickness rather than of badness. We rarely hold people responsible or accountable for their physical ills, and, although occasionally persons may not take the necessary precautions to avoid illness, we assume that illness happens to people, that it is not in their interest, and that it is, therefore, not motivated. For the community, difficulties in defining an act as sick or bad arise most frequently in the area of psychiatric disorders. Most psychiatrists take the position that many delinquents and criminals are sick rather than bad. But, although emotional difficulties can certainly be observed among such violators, we have difficulty establishing that the disturbing behavior is a result of the emotional makeup of the person rather than of some aspect of his social character. Because such attributions of cause can never be proved and because views in the community as to the most appropriate perspective for determining deviance conflict, the differences between violators sent to psychiatric institutions and those who find themselves in prisons are not so large as generally assumed. As the behavior and motivations of the individual become more bizarre and difficult to understand, we more readily apply the definition of sickness, but psychiatric conceptions of behavior include large residual categories such as the disordered personality and character disorders which clearly overlap with public and community conceptions of badness.

The tendency for mental patients to be viewed as being responsible for their condition, in contrast to the lack of attribution of such motives to the physically ill, explains in part the stigma associated with psychiatric disturbances. This stigma is also attributable to the fact that mental illness is frequently socially disruptive; it may threaten and frighten others, and it involves a large element of social unpredictability. Although some physical conditions on occasion lead to similar social problems, most persons who are physically ill do not threaten the community in the same way as do many psychiatric patients. Moreover, most people have at one time or another suffered from physical morbidity, and they recognize that becoming ill is a common occurrence. In contrast, they do not recognize themselves as having suffered from psychiatric conditions, and they do not necessarily accept the idea that people like themselves can become mentally ill.

The lack of correspondence in the public's attitudes toward physical and mental illness also stems in part from the common tendency to equate all mental illness with acute psychoses. A large proportion of the population conceives of the mental patient as being crazy, and they do not ordinarily think of the depressed person or the highly anxious or the withdrawn person as suffering from a psychiatric condition. Even many people who have been patients in mental hospitals, including those who have been admitted several times, fail to conceive of themselves as being mentally ill; frequently they characterize their difficulties in physical terms (Linn, 1968). In addition, unlike physical illness, mental illness is usually thought of by the public as characterizing the whole person rather than just one aspect of his functioning. The implication is that, because mental illness marks the entire person, he cannot be trusted to understand his situation or to make decisions concerning his welfare. This assumption is often untrue, and it is not difficult to understand why patients in mental hospitals wish to resist being viewed in this way.

In many ways the terms *psychiatric condition* and *mental illness* have become dysfunctional, especially when they are used to refer to a wide constellation of difficulties. These terms associate in the public mind any psychiatric difficulty with the stereotype of the severe psychoses and build an image of a person totally incapable of caring for himself. This image, shared by many patients as well, leads to resistance in accepting psychological problems and difficulties as being appropriate for psychiatric or psychological assistance. Given this profound barrier to receiving care, we might more reasonably view many people with psychiatric problems as having difficulties in interpersonal relations, as being inadequately trained, or as being deficient in social skills. To think of oneself as a person lacking particular skills is hardly so threatening to one's self-esteem as is thinking of oneself as a disordered personality. Similarly, the definition of a mental patient as a person having particular difficulty in getting along with others or as one who is particularly anxious when faced with certain situations is a familiar and acceptable view to the layman; and in any case such explanations are probably more comprehensible than are those implied by the actual definition of mental illness.

Views of Mental Illness in Relation to Social Policy

It is appropriate to inquire how varying mental health conceptions bear on the formulation of public policy. Although it is reasonable to maintain that if people need help it is the public's responsibility to provide it, whether or not it falls within the confines of mental illness, limitations always exist on the resources available. Decisions concerning how such resources are to be allocated among those who need help depend, therefore, on our conceptions of which problems constitute greater and lesser need.

Since optimal mental health is a utopian ideal, therapeutic programs always encounter never-ending layers of problems. Because the provision of services is one of the conditions affecting the demand for services, if the field is defined too broadly, infinite amounts of money, personnel, and time could theoretically be absorbed in providing mental health care. Resources, however, are never unlimited; we must weigh investments in mental health care against investments in education, transportation, recreation, housing, and the like; we must base such decisions on some concept of priorities and some notion of the criteria by which these priorities are to be established.

Priorities always depend on values; two paramount values are ordinarily applied in thinking about mental health needs. The first is a humanitarian value—the concept of need; it is based on the idea that the best services should be made available to those who need them despite the cost, the difficulty in obtaining them, or the pressure on resources. The second concept—the notion of gain—is based on the idea that services should be made available when the result achieved is equal to the investment. The widespread use of cost-benefit analysis has focused increasing attention on the concept of gain. This concept, however, clearly comes into conflict with humanitarian needs and values at some point, and so public policy usually involves some marriage, however uncomfortable, between the notions of need and of gain.

We can define the concept of need in terms of sickness and disability, and we can also view it from an economic perspective. Need depends on the severity of the condition in question and the amount of handicap it causes. The economic costs of reasonably dealing with severe and disabling psychiatric conditions are sufficiently large and sufficiently outside the income range of most of the mentally ill that the ability-to-pay criterion is largely irrelevant to the question of public responsibility.

From the perspective of cost-effectiveness (gain), several very different issues require resolution before an intelligent public policy can be formulated. The provision of services to the mentally ill and decisions regarding allocation of available resources should, in part, depend on the efficacy of alternative services, but such decisions are difficult to make. Vast investment in unproven and ineffective services may result in little gain beyond the humanitarian gesture of offering help to a person in need. Indeed, some services may harm the patient. For example, investments in psychodynamic psychotherapy—a very expensive service—are quite likely poor ones in contrast to investments in other less expensive means of helping the mentally ill since the efficacy of such therapy in rehabilitating patients is far from established. But frequently we just do not have sufficient data to make an informed assessment of the most reasonable directions for public programs.

Efficiency is also gained if the therapy provided not only cares for the illness when it occurs but also retards possibilities of remission or more extensive illness later on. Thus, all other factors constant (which they never are), we would expect curing the condition of a child or a young adult to result in continuing gains throughout the person's life. The same cure in the case of an older person would not produce an equal yield. Social values and humanitarian concerns often take precedence over the concept of gain, and thus services are provided in many situations on the basis of need, irrespective of cost-effectiveness. Utilizing the concept of gain too extensively obviously conflicts with a sense of compassion.

Major emphasis is now placed on providing preventive psychiatric services and early treatment on the assumption that such programs locate morbidity conditions early, retard continuing morbidity and disability, often prevent disability entirely, and stimulate positive mental health (Felix, 1967). We still cannot be sure, however, that we have the appropriate knowledge and skills to do all of these things effectively. Moreover, some preventive programs involve a high risk of iatrogenic illness—that is, morbidity which results from the services rendered rather than from the condition itself. Since many neurotic symptoms and fears are widely distributed and are transitory in nature, treating them as though they were aspects of emotional illness may encourage a feeling of helplessness in the patient. Such treatment may structure the symptom and the condition as part of his self-identity and discourage him from attempting to cope with and overcome his problem.

The conception of mental illness underlying public policy is important because different views suggest varying approaches to classifying psychiatric conditions and to caring for the patient. If we assume that psychological difficulties and problems are pervasive throughout the society and have always been so and that those who suffer from psychiatric disease are fundamentally different from the mass of people who have common psychological problems, we are in a very different position from one which states that mental illness is a continuum on which all these problems fall depending on their degree of seriousness.

Differing assumptions may lead to conflicting implications. For example, if one assumes a traditional Freudian position in regard to psychiatric illness, he tends to believe that personality is formed in early life and is not very susceptible to change from external environmental influences later on. However, a clinician working from the symbolic-interaction perspective, who believes that personality may constantly be modified by the environment and by the nature of an individual's associations, is more inclined than the Freudian to seek ways of changing the patient's current environment to achieve changes in his personality. The kinds of intervention attempted depend on the kinds of assumptions made about the nature of mental illness itself. On some occasions in the past for example, an organic view of mental illness prevented the provision of a healthy environment for the patient. Therefore, we must carefully consider the full implications of each of the relevant alternatives if we wish to understand the nature of the commitments we are making.

As mentioned above, because of limited resources and the need for priorities, we must assign some limits to the concept of psychiatric need. If mental illnesses are fundamentally different from ordinary problems in living and are defined not by social standards but by medical diagnoses of disease, public health policy should give highest priority to those patients who are clearly sick in a traditional psychiatric sense. Here we might assume on the basis of considerable evidence that many ordinary problems are transitory, while psychiatric disease states tend not to disappear so readily. Thus, public policy must give greatest emphasis to retarding and alleviating the disability of the chronically ill patient.

In contrast, if chronic mental illness and the psychoses are part of the same continuum as are other problems, we can treat all such conditions in fundamentally the same way—chronic disability is simply a manifestation of untreated and neglected illness. Indeed, early intervention may prevent chronic and severe mental illness. Moreover, if one accepts these assumptions—and they are assumptions rather than proven facts—it is reasonable to devote considerable resources to preventive work and to treating mild and moderate psychological disabilities.

One can understand the significance of these diverse approaches by looking at a difference of opinion that developed at a government-sponsored mental health conference. Alexander Leighton (1967), a professor of social psychiatry at the Harvard School of Public Health, took the position that mental disorders should be seen as part of a continuum.

> Typologies of this sort are able to handle the complex continuity that appears to exist between patterns of health and patterns of illness. One can picture this, diagrammatically, as comprising two extremes in a field: one side, health behaviors, is a dense population of white dots, and the other, psychiatric behavior (symptoms) is a dense population of black dots. As one looks across the field from light to dark, the whites grow less and less and the blacks become thicker and thicker. (p. 339)

Paul Lemkau (1967), professor of mental hygiene at Johns Hopkins, took strong exception to Leighton's formulation.

> We cannot properly look at our problem in this way, at least not all of our problems in this way; when we do so, we make the assumption almost automatically that the same kind of program will apply all the way across the board, all across these various shades of gray. All we need to do is to intensify or de-intensify a panacea-like program. I think this is false. I think it covers up the complexity of the task we have to do in therapeutic and preventive psychiatry. You don't cure phenylketonurie oligophrenia with psychotherapy, you prevent it by adjusting diet.
>
> Now I don't think that that fits in this scale of grayness. One can go on and on with these kinds of things and point out that the preventive and therapeutic programs are very large in number if we are going to fit the particular cases that, in reality, exist. I think Dr. Leighton does us a disservice when he tries to tell us that the matter is just gradations of the same thing. It isn't, and I don't think the *abandonment* of proper classification of illnesses is the answer to this kind of problem. (p. 363)

By drawing these positions sharply, we can exaggerate the extent to which two separate camps exist. Most mental health professionals are probably not clear about their views of mental illness or the assumptions which underly them. Usually they hold both opinions simultaneously, although the opinions themselves may be formally contradictory. Moreover, other complications bring the two views together. Moderate problems (even if they are not regarded as psychiatric illnesses) may become severe problems which incapacitate the individual in carrying out social roles. These serious problems are worthy of help regardless of whether they are part of the same order of phenomena as schizophrenia or other more traditionally recognized psychiatric conditions.

The development of a coherent and intelligent public policy depends partially on the perspectives taken but mostly on the resolution of specific empirical questions. What conditions and problems if they go untreated become chronic, and which ones are transitory? Obviously, no rational person would suggest that a large bulk of our medical resources be given to the treatment of the common cold since the condition is self-limited in any case. Similarly we must be able to identify psychiatric conditions analogous to the common cold. Moreover, we must be able to specify the effects of varying systems of intervention in psychiatric disturbances. Which social services and policies limit disability and handicap, and which ones exacerbate such problems? Do preventive psychiatric services increase the number of iatrogenic disturbances or encourage psychological hypochondriasis? How successful are preventive psychiatric services in insulating persons from future serious morbidity and disability? Although the answers to many of these questions are unknown, we must continue to ask them and to formulate them so that they are amenable to empirical investigation. Finally, although public policy must continue to develop despite the uncertainty of knowledge, the importance of such information should lead government agencies financing care to insist that serious attempts be made to evaluate program effectiveness.

The Patient and the Society: An Insoluble Dilemma

Because mental illness can be seen from many vantage points, the perspectives of the evaluators may come into conflict. Most commonly, observers view psychiatric difficulties either in terms of the psychological distress the person is experiencing or in terms of his social functioning. Although psychological comfort may contribute to adequate social functioning, these two aspects of adaptation are not necessarily brought about by the same conditions. Individuals and communities have long-range as well as short-range goals, and frequently they must incur psychological costs in the short run to achieve larger and more distant goals.

No society in history has been completely devoted to eliminating personal discomfort and pain. Usually we work to alleviate forms of distress that have no social function. Our most valued social institutions however do much to produce psychological stress, and we need go no further than the educational system to illustrate this point. University education frequently undermines students' most cherished beliefs; students are not infrequently failed in courses and dismissed from universities; and the educational system is always setting goals which some students cannot meet, resulting in a sense of failure and a loss of self-esteem. Implicit in the value structure of universities, however, is the idea that the incentives for performance or the need for acquisition of information and skills requires inducing some stress and personal pain into the student's life. Most societies operate on the premise that stress provides incentives and facilitates the development of important instrumental goals. Therefore, although it is often possible to relieve personal distress by reducing obligations and responsibilities, we frequently choose not to do so.

A major dilemma in psychiatry involves the emphasis to be placed on performance in contrast to that placed on the control of personal distress. Psychiatrists employed by particular institutions, such as the military, seek to minimize the number of psychiatric casualties from the perspective of social performance; but, no doubt, the performance is achieved at some cost to the psychological comfort of the people dealt with. When a time dimension is built into perspectives on mental health problems, such problems become even more complicated. The value of one alternative in relation to others depends obviously on the long-range goals of individuals and groups and on the extent to which societal pressures are necessary to achieve such goals. For example, if we minimize psychological distress at one stage in a person's life, at some cost to his performance and the extent to which he develops new skills, we may find at some later point that his lack of skills is an important cause of his difficulty and of the distress he experiences. On the other hand, if we neglect the issue of personal distress and place value only on the development of performance skills, we may "stress" a person to the extent that he is continuously uncomfortable, and he may refuse to function at all. In short, we must achieve some balance between mastery of the environment and individual comfort, not only for humanitarian reasons but also to facilitate continuing performance and mastery.

Social Problem or Mental Illness?

We have already reviewed the consequences of viewing disturbances in psychological functioning from the perspective of personality development in contrast to viewing them from a historical and social perspective. Although mental illness is clearly a social problem, it is not obvious which social problems fall within the domain of mental illness. Many Negroes, for example, suffer from a sense of inferiority and from other psychological difficulties, but to define such problems mainly from the psychiatric perspective neglects the societal and environmental problems that lead to the Negroes' distress. To treat the problems and neglect the issues is a disservice to the Negro and to society. Similarly, delinquency thrives in particular areas of large cities; to define delinquents as children in need of psychiatric care may direct us away from considering the social forces and conditions that lead to behavior defined by the larger society as unlawful. The concepts of mental health and mental illness are increasingly used ambiguously to include a wide range of social problems. These psychiatric definitions implicitly suggest that the individual is at fault, but many of these problems are a direct result of the organization and patterning of the community itself. Moreover, the implication also is that the proper means of changing these conditions is through changing the personalities and inclinations of individuals rather than through changing the structure of the society itself. Some mental health professionals believe, for example, that persons who illegally use drugs must be emotionally disturbed; it is equally plausible to consider whether certain laws pertaining to the use of specific drugs are truly consistent with scientific knowledge and, indeed, whether the inclination of many people to experiment with drugs is a reasonably normal response.

I do not mean to suggest that psychiatrists are unaware of the societal difficulties faced by the Negro or the social influences affecting delinquent behavior and the use of such drugs as marijuana among college students. But as long as the psychiatrist practices his craft, he inevitably approaches the problem from the viewpoint of changing the patient rather than changing the society. This contradiction has led some psychiatrists to reject traditional psychiatric roles and instead to direct themselves toward changing society itself. These new efforts are characterized as preventive psychiatry. But many psychiatrists have overreacted to their professional dilemma. In conceptually moving from the individual to the society they have argued that mental illness in general is a product of social forces and social structure and that the psychiatrist must concern himself with the community. This position will expand very widely the horizons of psychiatric work and the scope of psychiatric activity and places the psychiatrist in the political arena.

Another alternative to the psychiatric dilemma exists however. By noting that the problems of the Negro, the school dropout, the mother with illegitimate children, and the alienated student are rooted more in the influences and definitions of the society than in the conditions of individuals, we might appropriately conclude that such problems realistically are not the province of psychiatry at all, unless the person is also mentally ill in the more narrow sense. Each of these problems is most frequently associated with general conditions in the society rather than with specific conditions characterizing the person's inability to make an adequate adjustment without profound suffering. The psychiatrist, if he is to perform a specific function in society, cannot hope to be all things to all men. He must be trained to take on tasks in which he has a specific contribution to make and in which, indeed, the problems he works with are concentrated largely within individuals and their families. My view is that psychiatrists should have a particular function—to provide help to individuals who are disabled because they suffer from the specific kinds of problems which psychiatrists are uniquely trained to handle. There are many more such patients than psychiatrists can easily provide care for, and while psychiatrists have increased the scope of the problems they deal with in society, they have sadly neglected the patients suffering from more traditional psychiatric syndromes.

Psychiatric problems, of course, may contribute to larger social problems, and social problems may cause profound psychological distress. The issues which require clarification are whether it is reasonable or fruitful to treat most social problems as problems of mental health and whether the same professionals who are trained as experts in treating schizophrenia, depressive disorders, and other more typical psychiatric conditions are those who can most appropriately deal with problems resulting from environmental impoverishment, cultural deprivation, social change, economic and social discrimination, and other societal conditions. Since psychiatric manpower is very limited, investments in dealing with a wide range of social problems make inevitable the neglect of hard-core mental illness.

In raising such issues, I do not wish to imply that the society should not devote large resources to alleviating social problems and the many forms of inequality that exist. We must, however, entertain the hypothesis that in allowing the psychiatric perspective to muddy the social waters we may be diverting attention from more important questions involving both social problems and mental illness. Many of the major social problems we face require a large effort to develop an adequate system of social, economic, and educational services and opportunities available to all. The major problem of mental illness is to treat and, if possible, to prevent the psychological suffering and social handicaps evident among those so afflicted. Whether such problems are better attacked as separate questions or together is an important social-policy issue.

In suggesting that psychiatry, as a profession, might give greatest emphasis to the development of its specialized and traditional skills, I do not mean to indicate that the contexts for treating the mentally ill need be separated from contexts in which other medical and social difficulties are handled. Frequently the same patients may have a variety of difficulties and problems—some requiring psychiatric assistance, some requiring help from other professionals. On the whole it is desirable to coordinate and integrate the care such persons receive, both to facilitate their understanding of their needs and to allow professionals to provide the best overall program for their care and rehabilitation.

It is difficult to find agreement on policy questions pertaining to mental illness because different persons have varying conceptions of these disorders, and such conceptions determine in which direction it is most appropriate to move. We should therefore inquire more fully into the varying conceptions of the causes of mental illness and of measures which might alleviate the development of such conditions.

Chapter 3

CONCEPTIONS OF THE CAUSES OF AND MEANS OF CONTROLLING MENTAL ILLNESS

The dominant viewpoint in American psychiatry at the present time has two major premises. First, psychiatrists believe that the occurrence and prevalence of mental illness are directly related to social conditions, and thus that they must actively support policies aimed at improving the environment to a point where it becomes more conducive to mental health. Second, they assume that early intervention in the difficulties and social crises of individuals retards and alleviates future illness and disability (Caplan, 1964). Such viewpoints imply either that attempts to influence social policy on the one hand and to intervene in social crises on the other involve no social costs or that these costs are minimal in contrast to the large gains achieved. Each of these premises requires separate scrutiny.

The Impact of Environment on Mental Illness

Psychiatrists agree that environmental influences have an important impact on the development and course of some mental illnesses. They differ, however, in their theories of how environmental forces influence and interact with biological and personality influences. At one extreme stand those investigators who believe that a biological or a physiological defect is a necessary condition for mental illness and that psychiatric morbidity occurs only when persons with such inherited defects are faced with adverse circumstances which bring out their weaknesses. At the other extreme are those who see psychiatric morbidity as the result of compounded stresses and adverse environmental events.

In discussing the impact of environment on psychiatric conditions, one must separate the discussion of its effects in producing the primary condition from considerations dealing with the development of secondary disabilities (Lemert, 1951; Wing, 1962). Psychiatrists are aware that persons with the same condition—whatever its character—may suffer greater or lesser difficulty depending on the social and environmental circumstances to which they are exposed. While some investigators believe that social forces affect both the occurrence of the condition and the subsequent disability, others see the environment as important primarily in determining the extent of handicap. The scope of possibilities for preventive psychiatry depends, of course, on the extent to which environment actually affects psychiatric conditions.

Since it is impossible, given the state of our knowledge, to come to any definitive view on such issues, all I can do here is to present some of the contrasting positions concerning the etiology of mental conditions and develop some of the implications of each. Thus, I shall discuss in order the following perspectives: heredity, psychosocial development, learning, social stress, and societal reaction. Although I shall attempt to polarize these views to illustrate their distinctive aspects, it is important to recognize that most investigators adopt an eclectic view which synthesizes elements of each of these perspectives.

The Question of Inheritance and Environment

Although considerable controversy surrounds the validity of accepting a heredity hypothesis pertinent to schizophrenia and other mental disorders, this has been a dominant etiological approach. Various studies showing a higher concordance of schizophrenia among identical as opposed to fraternal twins provide a basis for these contentions. Although such studies have not yielded consistent results and have often included grave methodological errors (Jackson, 1960), the results obtained have provided as much basis for the heredity theory as there is for any other.

Evidence for a genetic etiology of schizophrenia also comes from studies comparing the offspring of schizophrenic parents with those of parents who were not mentally ill. L. Heston (1966), for example, compared the adjustment of 47 adults born to schizophrenic mothers with a matched control group of adults born to mothers who were not mentally ill. Those in both the subject and the control group in the study were separated from their natural mothers during the first few days of life and were reared during their early years in foster homes. The investigator found that the occurrence of schizophrenia and other pathologies was higher among the offspring of schizophrenic mothers than among the matched controls. Since the subjects of the study were removed from their schizophrenic mothers shortly after birth, we cannot conclude that the higher rate of pathology was a result of interaction with a schizophrenic mother. Such a study thus supports a hereditary etiology of schizophrenia. This theory, however, depends mostly upon studies of twins, and thus further consideration of the implications of such studies is necessary.

Perhaps most influential among the studies referred to above are those investigations carried out by Franz Kallman (1956). He found that while schizophrenic concordance varied from 10 to 18 per cent among fraternal twins, it was 78 to 92 per cent among identical twins. If we assume Kallman's findings to be correct, even though there are considerable inconsistencies among the findings of other studies of twins, they still leave room for positing factors other than genetic ones. If genetic factors were the only ones operating, the identical heredity of monozygotic twins would produce a perfect concordance rate.

Kallman felt there was no genetic reason why schizophrenia could not be seen from other perspectives as well. His position was that "a true schizophrenic psychosis is not developed under usual life conditions unless a particular predisposition has been inherited by a person from both parents" (p. 98), but that the disease resulted from the intricate interactions of genetic and environmental factors. He thus maintained that schizophrenia could be prevented or cured. Since environmental and psychosocial elements could predispose a person to, precipitate, or perpetuate psychoses, understanding of and control over such elements could retard the disease process.

Although theorists have analyzed this question extensively, they have not clearly defined the precise environmental factors contributing to a schizophrenic breakdown. Various evidence, however, shows that a psychotic breakdown is frequently preceded by a stressful event of some magnitude. G. W. Brown and J. L. P. Birley (1968), for example, in a study of 50 patients suffering from an acute onset or relapse of schizophrenia and a group of 377 normal controls, found that these groups differed in the proportion experiencing at least one major change in their lives in the 3-week period preceding investigation. While 60 per cent of the patient group had such an experience, only 19 per cent of the control group was so affected. Possibly, environmental stress leads to the initiation of treatment rather than to the illness itself, and persons similarly ill who do not suffer severe environmental stress are less likely to define themselves as requiring treatment. Since the condition studied, however, was a severe one, this interpretation probably does not explain the result obtained. This study is impressive in that the investigators separated the social changes into categories according to the extent to which the patient may have had control over them. The fact that the relationship held for events over which the patient had no control as well as for those he could affect supports the idea that this finding could not be simply explained by the argument that schizophrenic patients tend to get themselves into social difficulties because of their illness. The study suggests, in contrast, that significant changes in the patient's life affected adversely his psychological and social functioning. Other studies also suggest a relationship between the cumulation of stresses in a person's life and the occurrence of psychiatric morbidity, but the causal links in such relationships are not clearly understood (Langer et al., 1963).

Various theories attempt to explain the link between the occurrence of changes in a person's life and schizophrenic breakdown. One view is that those genetically predisposed to schizophrenia have nervous systems particularly vulnerable to the intense stimulation which social changes can bring. In this view a breakdown reflects the inability of the patient to tolerate a high level of stimulation. A second explanation for the increased vulnerability of schizophrenics to major changes and intense emotions involves the assumption that these conditions are threatening to persons who lack the ability to handle problems. Because of biological incapacities or inadequate social training, schizophrenics do not develop a repertoire of interpersonal techniques which allow them to face and deal with new and challenging situations. Therefore, they are more likely to suffer a breakdown in such circumstances. A third position is that schizophrenia is an adaptive attempt to meeting social adversity and difficulty, and although this approach has certain advantages, it results in disruptions as well.

Direction over environmental forces acting on the patient or on his capacity to tolerate or cope with particular changes may allow us to contain and to control illness and disability. The difficulty, however, is in specifying what particular environmental supports are most conducive to an optimal outcome. In the past, hospitals were much more willing to release schizophrenic patients who returned to family surroundings than they were to release those who had to make other living arrangements; but recent research suggests that particular family environments may not provide the best context for an optimal outcome (Freeman and Simmons, 1963; Carstairs, 1959). Whatever the final determination of such matters, mental health workers believe that schizophrenics and other mentally ill persons in the community require supportive care that helps them deal more fully with inevitable crises and that helps correct situations obviously detrimental to their future comfort and welfare.

The Psychosocial-Development Perspective

Most research in the mental health field is based on the premise that early psychosocial environment and family interaction are most influential in the development of personality and of mental disorders in later life. In the United States the importance of psychoanalytic and neopsychoanalytic theories of psychological and social development had a pervasive influence on the hypotheses developed and the research undertaken.

Intrinsic to the psychosocial approach is concern with how a child is socialized, how his parents react to his behavior, how they attempt to train him, and most importantly with the emotional tone of family interaction and of the relationships among the child, his siblings, and his peers. Among the variables frequently studied are the use of punishment by the parents, the degree of parental warmth, the dependency patterns in the family, the means of handling aggression, the forms of parental social control, and the family role structure (Maccoby, 1961).

In the study of schizophrenia, for example, several research groups have attempted to specify aspects of family functioning and relationships which predispose members to a schizophrenic reaction pattern. G. Bateson and his colleagues (1956) emphasize the idea of the double bind, a situation in which a person is subjected to incongruent or conflicting messages; the appropriate response is unclear, and the danger of being rebuked exists regardless of which message he responds to. Other investigators with a psychosocial perspective see schizophrenia as the confusion in identity resulting from distorted family role structures. T. Lidz (1963) and his associates describe two kinds of schizogenic families—one built around a sick, dominating parent, usually the mother, and the other characterized by chronic hostility among and mutual withdrawal of family members. Other approaches give primary emphasis to family interaction and communication, the organization of family role patterns and identities, and the peculiar use of sanctions (Mishler and Waxler, 1965).

Various investigators point to early peer relationships and adolescent problems in their attempts to explain schizophrenic conditions. Harry Stack Sullivan (1953), an important neo-Freudian theorist, emphasized the importance of preadolescence; during this period, he believed, the capacity to love matures. Sullivan theorized that this capacity is first developed through association with a chum of one's own sex. Such a relationship allows the preadolescent to see himself through others' eyes and provides him with consensual validation of his personal worth. During the adolescent period, the maturation of competence is particularly important; if a person can successfully negotiate this period, he can develop self-respect adequate to almost any situation. Such theories have encouraged various investigators to explore peer contacts and social isolation during adolescence in attempts to account for schizophrenic illness, but findings in this area have not been consistent. M. L. Kohn and J. A. Clausen (1955), for example, studied the childhood and adolescent social activities of schizophrenics and matched controls and found no support for the notion that social isolation during these periods brings about schizophrenia.

In general, although theorists are very interested in the psychosocial aspects of schizophrenia and other mental illnesses, they have little conclusive evidence on which to base preventive work. For the most part, the usual variances in child-rearing patterns appear to play a relatively small part in producing such profound difficulties as we are concerned with here; and, indeed, the relevance of different child-rearing practices in personality development in general is far from established. Any relatively warm, accepting family climate which nurtures a sense of self-esteem in the child and provides training experiences not too far out of touch with social realities will probably produce a "normal" child. Despite the earlier theoretical assumptions which perpetuated the myth of the fragile child, children are exceedingly flexible and adaptive, and relatively strong and invulnerable to modifications in their environments. Indeed, adversity in childhood may lead to the development of mastery and strength. The contexts which appear to breed pathology are those which are emotionally bizarre or deprived and in which the child experiences profound rejection, hostility, and other forms of social and emotional abuse as well as being exposed to inadequate, ineffective, and incongruous models of behavior.

From a preventive point of view there are several theoretical possibilities, although they are extremely difficult to implement. We generally recognize that brutal, dehumanizing environments such as are characteristic of urban slums do little to promote healthy, constructive family life. But such issues as altering living patterns, improving housing conditions, eliminating social discrimination, and providing good schools are very much intertwined with political and social processes, and society probably will not alter its priorities and decisions merely because mental health workers feel that current conditions may lead to poor mental health. These and similar battles, if they are to be fought at all, must be fought in the political realm—a realm in which mental health workers have demonstrated no special ability. If, indeed, mental health workers cannot be particularly influential in altering the political structure, then they must devote their efforts to repairing whatever damage societal conditions have created.

The usual approach taken by workers with a psychosocial perspective is to alter individual family conditions and understandings which they believe are not conducive to the mental health of the members (see Bolman and Westman, 1967). They contend that encouraging people to seek supportive help and counseling when difficulties and crises first occur, alleviates problems and avoids in these families future complications and difficulties conducive to morbidity. Family problems and patterns of interaction however are frequently very hard to solve or alter. Mental health workers are not at all sure just what aspects of family functioning are central to the morbidity condition. Also, the therapeutic relationship, even if properly directed and effectively organized, constitutes such a small part of family interaction that it may not be able to overcome the more common experiences family members have with one another and with their community. Finally, we cannot always separate those aspects of family interaction that were conducive to family pathology in the first place and those that constitute adaptive responses to the presence of pathology. The frequent occurrence of a dominant mother and a weak, withdrawing father in families with a great variety of social and psychiatric problems suggests that such family structures may be a reaction to sickness in one of the members rather than an important cause.

In a study involving the use of child-guidance facilities at a well-known mental hospital, Shepherd and his colleagues (1966) matched children being treated with other children having similar problems who were not receiving treatment. Varying needs of the parents and their patterns of illness behavior accounted for the fact that some children were treated but others with identical problems were not. When they reevaluated the treated and untreated groups of children 2 years later, the investigators found little difference in their rates of improvement. Moreover, even within the treated group the amount of improvement was unrelated to the amount of treatment provided. Approximately two-thirds of both groups of children—treated and untreated—had improved in the 2-year period. How are we to interpret these findings?

The investigators concluded that many of the symptoms treated were no more than temporary exaggerations of reaction patterns occurring normally in human development. They believe that clinicians who have concentrated on morbidity have an incomplete appreciation of the normal range of reaction patterns and, thus, give exaggerated significance to symptoms and problems which are not really pathological and which do not ordinarily require treatment (also see Robins, 1966, pp. 300–303). Those more skeptical about such studies point out an important differentiating factor between the treated and untreated groups. The fact that some children were brought into treatment suggests that their parents were either unable or unwilling to cope with their problems, and the findings suggest that such parents also had fewer resources for dealing with the difficulties of their children. Thus, since these children did no worse than those whose parents had effective coping resources, therapy may have been helpful and effective. The data on hand do not really allow us to conclusively evaluate the opposing arguments. However, even if we accept the argument of the proponents of child therapeutic services, the outcomes achieved by such services are at best extremely modest. We, therefore, must be willing to consider the possibility of using equivalent resources in a manner encouraging a larger and more effective return.

In discussing the problem of psychosocial approaches to mental disorder in such general terms, I do not wish to suggest that researchers and therapists assuming this perspective are of one mind. In this section I have directed attention primarily to those approaches based on the assumption that it is important for the patient to appreciate the nature of his social relationships as well as his psychological and social inclinations. In the following section we shall consider orientations which have psychosocial aspects but which do not necessarily require that the patient appreciate his situation.

The Learning Perspective

Over the years psychologists have achieved substantial understanding of the learning process. Although some early attempts were made to translate these findings into a therapeutic approach, only recently have such attempts become a major investment and an enterprise of some importance in therapeutic research.

One of the first systematic attempts to link learning theory and psychoanalytic practice was presented in a book written by J. Dollard and N. E. Miller in 1950. In *Personality and Psychotherapy* the authors brought together the formulations of Hullian learning theory and various psychoanalytic concepts and tried to specify the conditions under which habits are formed and changed. They reformulated various psychoanalytic concepts such as the unconscious, conflict, and repression into stimulus-response terms using the concepts of drive, cue, response, and reward. For example, they pointed out that repression is the learned avoidance of certain thoughts. Because some thoughts arouse fear (a secondary drive stimulus), ignoring them leads to drive reduction and to reinforcement; in this way the response becomes a learned part of a person's repertoire.

Although various efforts to analyze psychotherapeutic processes within a learning frame of reference continued, a book by J. Wolpe (1958), *Psychotherapy by Reciprocal Inhibition,* gave considerable impetus to the use of learning theory in psychotherapy. Wolpe maintained that psychotherapeutic effects were produced mainly by complete or partial suppression of anxiety responses by the simultaneous evocation of other responses physiologically antagonistic to anxiety. Wolpe maintained that neurotic behavior is a persistent but learned and unadaptive anxiety response acquired in anxiety-generating situations. Such anxiety responses are unadaptive because they are manifest in situations which contain no objective threat. Given these assumptions, Wolpe and others have developed therapeutic approaches, such as desensitization, relaxation, and operant conditioning, different from those ordinarily practiced.

The learning approaches to psychotherapy, or what is more commonly called behavior therapy, are based on the idea that it is possible to develop reinforcement schedules which weaken unadaptive responses and reinforce more adaptive behavior. This approach is specifically directed toward changing particular aspects of the person rather than toward such ambitious but unrealistic results as psychic reintegration.

Critics of behavior therapy charge that such procedures may change symptoms but that they are not directed toward basic causes. They also maintain that except for very specific conditions, such as phobias and sexual impotence, which are dominated by a single symptom, mental conditions are characterized by very complicated syndromes for which it is very difficult to discern and develop specific reinforcement schedules or other remedial procedures. They argue that one must understand the relevant, important cues and stimuli in the patient's illness before proceeding; but more frequently than not learning these requires a long period of therapeutic work.

The contention that behavior therapy just reduces particular symptoms or substitutes one for another is hardly a valid criticism. Implicit in it is the assumption that a more basic cure is possible but little evidence supports such a claim. Changing destructive, specific patterns of behavior such as self-mutilation or fear of leaving one's house is anything but trivial. The second argument, concerning the difficulty of locating specific cues and the patterns of behavior and thinking to which they are associated, points to a more serious problem and one which may limit the usefulness of behavior therapy. But if we are to evaluate behavior therapy, we must consider the success of its techniques in treating what it purports to treat. Because it is probably more useful in some cases than in others, we must consider how it compares in each specific instance with the other forms of therapy available.

It is too early to assess in any general way the usefulness and effectiveness of behavior therapy. Most comparisons of behavior therapy with other modes of treatment are not based on carefully controlled evaluations. Yet, behavior therapy, at least in specific instances, seems somewhat more effective than more traditional forms of psychotherapy (Eysenck and Rachman, 1965). Work with autistic children and with very specific neurotic conditions has had particularly promising results.

Behavior therapy is not really a preventive approach within the terms of our discussion in this chapter. In its preventive aspects, however, it clarifies the importance, as do other approaches, of early conditioning and appropriate social reinforcements. Its underlying theory is that un-adaptive behavior is in large part learned and can be prevented by having appropriate social structures. (Skinner, 1962).

The Social-Stress Perspective

Although the social-stress perspective is not based on an elaborate theory or concept, it is increasingly used as a rationale for public policy in the mental health field. In one sense it is the most simple of the perspectives involving mental health, but at the same time it poses some of the most difficult scientific dilemmas. (For the most comprehensive available discussion of the stress perspective, see Lazarus (1966).)

Stated simply, the social-stress perspective assumes that every person has his breaking point and that mental illness and psychiatric disability are products largely of the cumulation of stress in people's lives; this stress eventually overcomes their coping abilities (Langer, *et al.*, 1963). This assumption is the basic rationale of military psychiatry, and in recent years it has been applied as well to the preventive and community psychiatric movements, and particularly to community mental health clinics. It is essential to recognize that in the application of this perspective clear distinctions are not drawn between psychoses and other kinds of problems causing psychological and social disability; very great weight is given to the idea that mental illness is environmentally caused.

An important preventive measure follows directly from the social-stress approach. If social stress is so severe that it taxes people's coping abilities and causes psychiatric disability, then supportive therapies which help alleviate stress or which buck up coping efforts are worthwhile. Thus, military psychiatry provides support and encouragement to soldiers who no longer feel willing or able to handle fear, anxiety, or other forms of psychological discomfort. Similarly, community agencies may provide support for patients who are distressed. If the stress can be alleviated to some extent, the resources patients have may allow them to continue functioning without breakdown. Such therapy attempts to enhance the client's social and psychological resources through instruction, support, encouragement, and at times even intimidation.

The so-called crisis therapies provide such support when it is believed patients are particularly vulnerable to disrupted functioning. The value of such therapies is difficult to determine since no careful comparative studies of such care in contrast to other forms of care are available. Moreover, the criteria to be used in judging such efforts are not established. We can understand this dilemma more easily if we look carefully at the military case and consider its relevance to the civilian situation.

The military mental health worker is an agent of the military rather than an agent of the soldier. His major function is to help ensure that psychiatric disability is minimized and military performance maximized. Thus, he is primarily concerned with maintaining the soldier as a functioning member of the unit and is only incidentally concerned with the soldier's mental health or happiness. He attempts to locate those who are unlikely to function adequately and to see that such men are quickly separated from the service. He pressures those who are kept on to continue functioning whatever the ultimate cost to their happiness or mental health, since the military goal of effective performance is enhanced by such a policy. In contrast, the civilian mental health worker has no such clear definition of his task. Although their roles are increasingly becoming confused, such civilian workers usually function as agents of the patient. In this case, effective performance is not clearly more laudable than are the competing goals of psychological comfort, desire for the secondary advantages resulting from lowered performance expectations, or long-range performance. When a military psychiatrist faces a man who is reluctant to fulfill combat expectations because he fears dying, the psychiatrist's responsibility is clear; but the civilian psychiatrist cannot be so sure of his responsibility since he knows that his patient's desire to avoid military obligations may very well save his life.

The basic assumption underlying the stress perspective is more questionable than it may appear. Although persons who have considerable stress in their lives are more likely than those with less stress to be psychologically distressed and disabled, psychotic conditions, particularly schizophrenia, are not more prevalent under stressful circumstances. Contrary to popular conceptions, war, urban living, and the hectic pace of modern life do not have any important effect on the occurrence of psychoses,* although they do affect how the community deals with the mentally ill (see Goldhamer and Marshall, 1953; Reid, 1961; Group for the Advancement of Psychiatry, 1960; Fried, 1964; and Murphy, 1961). In contrast, some evidence suggests that stressful conditions of living increase nervousness and anxiety and that modern life may increase loneliness and a sense of alienation. We may perhaps wish to devote our preventive re-

---

* In general, little evidence supports the contention that economic fluctuations affect the incidence of mental illness. However, a recent study by M. H. Brenner (1967) of the relationship from 1910 to 1960 between admissions to New York State mental hospitals and the state's employment index shows an inverse relationship. His data, however, are not subject to clear interpretation. Among the possible factors producing the observed correlation are: the influence of economic stress in precipitating illness, the increased intolerance of deviance during periods of economic hardship, the use of mental hospitals to shelter unfortunates during periods of economic stress, and the use of mental hospitals as an almshouse during periods of economic depression. For an excellent review of studies on the effects of social change on mental health, see Fried (1964).

sources to these latter problems, but we ought to be sufficiently clear that such an approach may not have any important influence on hard-core mental illness.

If we assume, for the purpose of argument, that preventive and community psychiatry should attack stress-related symptoms and general societal malaise, we still must decide whether this goal can be achieved by the programs envisioned. I have already pointed out that the success of crisis therapies and supportive care can be evaluated only through careful studies comparing these programs with other forms of care—and such studies are as yet unavailable.

Even if such programs were successful, they would not really be preventive according to those psychiatrists who wish to influence and change the societal forces which produce stress and unhappiness. We must evaluate such aspirations in terms of their scientific merit as well as of their political feasibility. It is a commonplace observation that deviant behavior, alienation, and unhappiness are often consequences of the structure of society itself: the stratification system, the distribution of wealth, the conflicting goals and interests, the quality of the environment, and so on. It is often argued that if we knew how to change the environment effectively and to deal with such problems as inequality, poverty, and misuse of power, deviant response could be greatly alleviated if not eliminated.

Even if we had complete power to change society, however, it is presumptuous to believe that we have the knowledge to bring about the results we desire. Other societies have attempted to develop social structures which eliminate the forces that produce deviant behavior. Those who planned the British National Health Service, for example, naïvely believed that, as good health service became available to the population, illness would slowly disappear and the costs of the health service would continuously decrease. The absurdity of this view is now apparent for we well know that the provision of medical services has only a small relationship to the occurrence of illness and that demand for new medical services develops as supply increases. Similarly, the Soviet Union tried to develop a social structure that eliminated forces producing deviant behavior; it is obvious that the venture failed—at least from this perspective. Despite the fantastic complexity of social structures, many naïve analysts have the notion that they could solve the problems of mental health if only they had the power. Even if mental health workers had the expertise necessary to convert social structures so that such structures facilitated mental health, they would not be given the power to do so because mental health goals and the changes necessary to implement them come into conflict with other social goals and values which have equal if not higher priority.

One regrettable conclusion often drawn from the stress perspective is that mental health is facilitated by insulating persons from the stressful and difficult circumstances which tax their resources. While it is true that stress so overwhelming that it defeats people in fulfilling their goals is not conducive to health, difficult and adverse life circumstances are not necessarily destructive to human personality. Persons develop skills and resources by facing difficulties and overcoming them. They develop strengths through experience and practice. If such capacities are not taxed, they do not develop and improve. In any system that strives to instill a high level of skill and mastery, some failures in achievement and performance inevitably result. Such failures may be the price required for maintaining a society which nurtures and develops skilled performance. Although any humanitarian society concerns itself with the problems of those who do not achieve success, such a society may not seek to eliminate stress itself.

The Societal-Reaction Perspective

The societal-reaction perspective is concerned less with the origins of deviant response and more with those social forces which help structure, organize, and perpetuate such reactions. Advocates of this perspective argue that deviant response is reinforced and perpetuated by social reactions to it, by the manner in which it is labeled, and by the resultant exclusion and discrimination against the deviant. The basic assumptions underlying this approach are that each society produces its own deviants by its definitions and rules and that such processes of definition help maintain the boundaries of the society (Lemert, 1951; Erickson, 1966).

The model most usually presented is a sequential one in which over time a pattern of deviant response is labeled in a fashion which increases the probability that further similar responses will occur (Becker, 1963). As the definition of the deviant response persists and as normal roles become more difficult for the deviant to assume because of limited opportunities and growing exclusion, his deviant acts become organized as part of his social identity and as an ongoing deviant role. Thus, the labeling process itself helps convert transitory, common deviant behavior into a more stable pattern of persistent deviant response.

In the case of mental illness, for example, T. Scheff (1966b) argues that such disorders are residual forms of deviant behavior for which we have no other appropriate labels and that such behaviors arise from fundamentally diverse sources. He argues that the occurrence of such symptoms or deviant responses is frequent and is usually neither labeled nor defined. Since such behavior occurs within normal and conventional response repertoires, it usually is temporary and nonpersistent. However, when such behavior is explicitly identified and labeled, the forces produced help organize the behavior into a social role. Scheff hypothesizes that, although deviants do not explicitly learn the role of the mentally ill, they are able to assume it because they have learned stereotyped imagery from early childhood of what mental illness is; the movies, television, radio, newspapers, and magazines inadvertently but continuously support and supplement this imagery. Scheff believes that deviants labeled as mentally ill may receive a variety of advantages by assuming the role and enacting it, although their assumption of the role need not be a conscious process. He argues that when such persons attempt to return to normal, conventional roles, their opportunities are restricted, and they may be punished as a result of the stigma associated with their past difficulties. They often have problems in obtaining adequate employment and difficulties in interpersonal affairs because they have been classified as mentally ill. As Scheff sees it, the transition from mental symptoms as an incidental aspect of social performance to mental illness as a social role occurs when the individual is under considerable personal and social stress. In such circumstances, the person may himself accept the societal definition of his status and develop a deviant concept of his identity.

Although the societal-reaction approach is provocative and obviously identifies processes that occur to some extent in the definition and care of mental patients, the relative importance of such processes is not clearly established. No one would deny that social labels can have powerful effects on individuals, but little evidence suggests that such labeling processes are sufficiently powerful to be major influences in producing chronic mental illness. Obviously, the labeling process is not sufficient in itself to produce mental illness, yet existing theories of societal reaction are extremely vague in defining clearly the conditions under which labeling will or will not produce deviant behavior. Some patients get well rather quickly and stay well, while others, such as schizophrenics, tend to be chronically ill; the theory of labeling does not explain why such differences occur.

Regardless of the vagueness of the societal-reaction approach, it does alert us to possible significant areas of preventive psychiatry. It suggests that the manner in which treatment resources define and deal with persons may either encourage sick-role behavior or prevent it. The expectations we communicate to the mentally ill are important. From a preventive point of view this perspective suggests that we should communicate the expectation that they can continue to function in conventional social roles and the belief that their difficulty is a problem in living or communication rather than a personal pathological state.

In its most extreme form the societal perspective suggests that if we ignore deviant behavior it will not persist. This, of course, is an absurd conclusion unless we mean by it that, if we do not define certain patterns of behavior as problems, then they are not problems. The real question is how to define deviant behavior in a manner which decreases the probability of its persistence and ensures the least disruption of the community and of individual personalities.

The Limitations of Psychotherapy

The term *psychotherapy* encompasses diverse activities based on such a wide variety of theories and ideas that it refers to little more than a social relationship between a therapist and a patient structured to improve the patient's perspective or condition. The rules governing the relationship, the goals envisioned, and the methods used may vary widely from one therapist to another and even within therapeutic relationships ostensibly based on the same theory and approach. Moreover, psychotherapies differ in length and frequency, directiveness, degree to which the therapist participates in an overt way, and emphasis on the past versus the present.

Even if we recognize psychotherapy as a solution to psychiatric problems, it is not a feasible approach for most of the patients who require help. Most approaches to psychotherapy require a relatively intensive and long-term relationship between a patient and a therapist. Thus they involve prohibitive monetary cost, and they require a vast number of therapeutic personnel. Moreover, many therapists believe that the skills required to engage in a successful psychotherapeutic relationship are not characteristic of lower socioeconomic groups; these groups, however, have the highest prevalence of psychiatric problems (Hollingshead and Redlich, 1958; Dohrenwend, 1966). Thus, psychotherapy is not a satisfactory approach on which to base public policy.

Since the goals of psychotherapy vary so widely, it is difficult to know which criteria are appropriate for evaluating its efficacy. From the perspective of public policy, a reasonable goal would be to reduce personal distress and to promote successful social functioning, but psychotherapists may see their goal as uncovering repressed needs and desires or making unconscious ideas conscious. Other therapists, in contrast, may emphasize the resocialization of the patient or the reconditioning of particular patterns of behavior. They may visualize their therapies as helping the patient to achieve self-realization or a better understanding of the social games in which he is involved. Frequently, psychotherapists do not disclose their goals at all, or they may specify them in only a very general and ambiguous manner.

If one argues, as Thomas Szasz (1965b) does, that psychotherapy is an educational experience in which the therapist helps the patient appreciate his range of personal choices and no more, then whether the patient feels better or shows a better adjustment to his milieu is irrelevant to the evaluation of psychotherapy. Most psychiatrists, however, view therapy as treatment for curing or improving the patient's condition, and thus we must evaluate these therapies in terms of these goals. This is not an appropriate context for reviewing the many studies, discussions, and debates concerning the effectiveness of psychotherapy. We should note, however, the vast disagreement concerning psychotherapeutic effectiveness; no strong evidence justifies public support for the expansion of this form of service. We have few well-designed studies of psychotherapy; and we can criticize almost every investigation on one basis or another. But the over-all conclusion one draws from most of the investigations that attempted to have an adequate methodology is that psychotherapy is not very different in its effectiveness from many less costly procedures such as bed rest, simple interpersonal support, and being on a patient waiting list (Eysenck, 1965). Although the matter is far from closed, the success of traditional psychotherapy as a treatment technique seems at best equivocal. Developments in the area of behavior therapy—treatment directed at specific symptoms and based on principles of learning theory—appear more promising (Eysenck and Rachman, 1965; Wolpe, 1966). Even if behavior therapy fulfills its promising forecast however, it will still fall far short of dealing with the large variety of problems and disabilities toward which mental health services are oriented.

I do not mean to debate the fact that many patients who enter traditional psychotherapy feel better and experience some improvement in various facets of their lives. However, many patients not receiving such care also improve. Many psychiatric problems are self-limited, and others respond to many varieties of support. Some analysts argue that the similarity in reported rates of success among therapies that radically differ suggests that patient improvement can be explained largely by techniques common to most therapies: suggestion, facilitation, encouragement, and support (Frank, 1961).

In discussing the question of effectiveness we must recognize the difficulty of evaluating various psychotherapies. Even if we attribute psychotherapeutic effects to suggestion and support (and many therapists would deny such an attribution), people are not equally suggestible in response to the same situation. While some find sustenance in their religious beliefs and others respond to faith healing, still others may require a particularly sophisticated kind of faith healing. Those drawn to psychotherapy in the first place may be a specially selected group who cannot benefit from the institutional sources of support and encouragement which are of help to other people.

Regardless of how one feels about traditional forms of psychotherapy, its effects are too limited and unimpressive and the expense of instituting it on a far-reaching basis is too great in terms of cost and personnel to justify it. Although older forms of psychotherapy will no doubt persist and new ones develop, at most psychotherapy will play only a limited role in the future organization of psychiatric rehabilitation.

In this chapter and in the previous ones I have tried to illustrate the difficulties in defining clearly the realm of mental illness, the varying conceptions of this phenomenon, its underlying etiological viewpoints, and its implications for possible preventive work. Having raised some of the important theoretical issues, we will now look into specific matters concerning mental health policies and the development of mental health services.

Chapter 4

THE DEVELOPMENT OF MENTAL HEALTH POLICY IN THE UNITED STATES

Stimulated by government interest and funding, mental health care has been changing rapidly, and discussions of the role of psychiatric care are increasingly directed to new organizational forms for caring for the mentally ill. In planning for the future we can often obtain insights from the past and, therefore, we should attain some perspective on events that have already occurred and on the social, cultural, and ideological forces that have influenced them.

Mental illness is not a new problem; the mentally ill have always existed in society. Moreover, methods of caring for the mentally ill have not followed a consistent developmental pattern; rather they have been characterized by stops and starts, by advances and setbacks. Indeed, much of our present conception of mental illness and many current proposals not only were advocated but also were practiced a century ago. Milieu treatment, a concept widely popular today, existed in the nineteenth century in both Europe and America under the rubric of moral treatment. Moral treatment was based on the assumption that psychiatric illness could be alleviated if the patient was treated in a considerate and friendly fashion, if he had the opportunity to discuss his troubles, if his interest was stimulated, and if he was kept actively involved in life. Close relationships between staff and patients often prevailed, and patients were treated in a personal and sympathetic fashion. In the passage that follows, a doctor in New York State writing in 1911 describes his conception of moral treatment.

> [It] consists in removing patients from their residence to some proper asylum; and for this purpose a calm retreat in the country is to be preferred: for it is found that continuance at home aggravates the disease, as the improper association of ideas cannot be destroyed. . . . Have humane attendants, who shall act as servants to them; never threaten but execute; offer no indignities to them, as they have a high sense of honour. . . . Let their fears and resentments be soothed without unnecessary opposition; adopt a system of regularity; make them rise, take exercise and food at stated times. The diet ought to be light, and easy of digestion but never too low. When convalescing, allow limited liberty; introduce entertaining books and conversation. (Quoted in Deutsch (1949), pp. 91–92.)

The idea of moral treatment is attributed to the French physician Philippe Pinel, who broke the pattern of harsh custodialism associated with mental institutions and substituted a program based on kindness and sympathy. It was not difficult to demonstrate that mental patients respond to sympathy and care, and Pinel had a profound influence on psychiatrists not only in Europe but also in America. Pinel's program was based on his belief that psychological factors were important causes of emotional disturbances, as were social factors and an inadequate education. Treatment of the insane, he believed, was only a form of education, and intelligent understanding associated with a minimum of mechanical restraint would bring good results.

Although moral treatment was established at institutions throughout the world, the sense of social responsibility toward the unfortunate which is increasingly being developed today was not very strong, and most patients received no better care than they had previously. Mental patients were undifferentiated for the most part from the destitute poor; and when moral treatment was practiced, it was available mainly to relatively affluent persons. Dorothea Dix, a New England spinster who became concerned about the inhumane care received by most of the mentally ill, was able to rally influential persons to her support in initiating a reform movement which had a great effect on developments in the nineteenth century. This movement was directed to improving the care of those mentally ill paupers who were severely punished for their condition or who received no care at all. It is ironic that this reform movement, inspired by lofty motives, led in the United States and elsewhere to the development of large custodial institutions which have set the tone for the care of the mentally ill to the present day. Although some smaller institutions practicing moral treatment existed at the time, for the most part the impoverished mentally ill were excluded from them. Dorothea Dix's movement thus was directed toward providing a minimum amount of help, and this was a significant advance in the care of the mentally ill at the time. Events later proved that, once a particular system of care had developed, it was enormously difficult to alter it.

Even the institutions for the more fortunate that practiced moral treatment were not immune to social changes. The industrial revolution in America, accompanied by changing conditions and growing immigration, led to an increased tendency to hospitalize those who could not adapt to their new circumstances (Grob, 1966). While industrialization was leading to increasing intolerance for peculiar and bizarre behavior, the unfortunate were exposed to great difficulties in the new urban environment. Life was particularly harsh for the unskilled immigrants, who experienced the misery characteristic of the industrial working class of the time. It was often such persons who exhibited bizarre and disorganized patterns of behavior. This combination of unfamiliar cultural patterns and bizarre behavior led to growing feelings that the mentally ill should be removed from the community and to increased demands on the existing mental hospitals to accommodate them. With the limited facilities and resources available mental hospitals dealt with the demand by regimentation of patients and development of bureaucratic procedures. There were, of course, variations from area to area and among different kinds of hospitals; any general attempt to depict the climate throughout the entire United States would be inadequate. Studies of individual hospitals, however, provide a picture of some of the social forces and ideological influences that affected the structure of mental hospitals; we now turn to a review of the early history of one such hospital.

The Early History of Worchester State Hospital

In a sophisticated history Gerald Grob (1966) traces the various social forces that affected the growth and the organization of Worchester State Hospital, established in 1830 as the first state hospital for the mentally ill in Massachusetts. The interest in a mental hospital in Massachusetts was encouraged by the inadequacy of informal methods of caring for the indigent and insane and was activated by vigorous, enlightened reformers who were motivated by a strong sense of religious and social responsibility. The new hospital in its earliest period (1833–1846) practiced moral treatment and offered its patients an optimistic and humanitarian climate. Early records of the hospital suggest considerable success at rehabilitation, not because of the efficacy of any particular psychiatric treatment, but probably as a result of the hopeful and encouraging climate, which supported the patient and inspired a feeling in him of being helped. Moral treatment, however, did not persist, and for most of the nineteenth century the hospital was guided by a pessimistic psychiatric ideology that mirrored its custodial nature.

As Grob shows so well, the organization of psychiatric care was responsive to social, economic, and ideological influences in the society at large. Industrial and technological change in Massachusetts, coupled with increasing immigration and urbanization, brought decreasing tolerance for bizarre and disruptive behavior and less ability to contain deviant behavior within the existing social structure. The general contempt of Massachusetts society for the Irish immigrants, who constituted a growing proportion of the insane, led to increasing pressures on the mental hospital to take on many new patients. With the growing number of patients —the mass of them held in low esteem by the community as well as by mental hospital personnel—it was impossible to maintain the administrative and environmental attitudes necessary for moral treatment. Moreover, with a growing number of patients and limited resources, it was necessary to develop more efficient custodial attitudes and procedures. The contempt in which the hospital held its clients and the low social value accorded them by the society at large neither stimulated hospital administrators to demand greater resources to care for their patients nor encouraged the community to provide further and more intensive support.

But other forces as well led to the deterioration of the hospital. As Grob argues, new psychiatric ideologies and professionalization among psychiatrists did much to retard the care of the mentally ill. These ideologies were in part the product of the psychiatrist's own attitudes and beliefs, molded by his social background and influenced by his need to maintain and increase his status and position. Grob believes that psychiatric insistence that the profession was scientific exerted a negative effect on mental hospitals. The emphasis on somatic factors within the traditional medical model had little to offer in the treatment of patients, and it undermined alternative approaches which could have produced improvement in patients by communicating a sense of confidence and hope (also see Bockoven, 1957). Furthermore, he argues that the development of a professional psychiatric subculture erected barriers between psychiatrists and other groups and was used to justify the exclusion of laymen who had provided much of the impetus for the improvement of mental health care. Finally, the trend toward professionalism isolated psychiatrists from the more humanitarian and compassionate ideologies existing in the society and replaced these with a barren, alleged objectivity which offered little help or hope. Professionalization of psychiatrists thus hampered the administration of psychiatric care.

More Recent Developments in Mental Health Policy

American psychiatry and mental health policy, as we know them today, are for the most part post-World War II developments. At the beginning of World War II there were only 3,000 psychiatrists in the United States, and shortages among other treatment and research personnel in the mental health field were even more acute. Although the manpower shortage persists in mental health, progress is reflected in the fact that as of December 31, 1964, 17,047 psychiatrists were actively practicing in the United States. Even more impressive increases have occurred in psychology, psychiatric nursing, psychiatric social work, and other mental health fields.

Except for its traditional role in mental hospitals, the profession of psychiatry became most extensively involved in public policy issues during World War II, initially through its participation in selective-service screening. Between January 1942 and June 1945, an estimated 1,875,000 men among the 15 million men examined were rejected for service because of alleged psychiatric disabilities. Of the men inducted, a large proportion of those later separated from the armed forces on a disability charge were discharged specifically for neuropsychiatric reasons (Felix, 1967, pp. 28–29). These facts alone created great concern and stimulated interest in improving basic preventive and treatment services and research in the psychiatric area.

In noting the influence of such involvement, we should also point out that psychiatric participation in selective service was less successful than one might have anticipated, given the claims of its advocates. Partly because of the shortage of adequately trained professionals, partly because of the meager development of psychiatric criteria for screening, and partly because of the way selective service was administered under the pressure of manpower requirements, such screening was for the most part a failure (see Ginzberg *et al.*, 1959). Albert Deutsch (1949) describes the situation in this way:

> It had been recommended that one psychiatrist be assigned to draft examining boards for every fifty registrants, and that a minimum of fifteen minutes be devoted to every psychiatric examination. When the many millions began to pour through selective service centers, however, these proposals became scraps of paper on the wind. Instead of fifteen minutes, an average of barely two minutes was devoted to the psychiatric examination of Army recruits. It was not unusual for a single psychiatrist to examine 200 men daily. The course of psychiatric screening throughout the war was highly irregular. In some states and in some centers, men with long mental hospital records were rushed into the armed forces; in many centers, no effort was made to ascertain institutional histories for psy-

chotic episodes; at others, men with histories of very mild emotional disorders were summarily rejected. The pendulum of directives swung from one extreme to another during the war; at one period, practically everybody not obviously psychotic was accepted for service; at another, nobody with the slightest trace of neurosis passed the examining board. (p. 463)

It would be totally inappropriate to evaluate, as some have attempted, the possibilities for psychiatric screening on the basis of the selective-service experience. As Deutsch points out, the conditions under which these psychiatric examinations took place were totally unrealistic. Moreover, these examinations were frequently undertaken by general physicians with little or no training in psychiatry. However, one important observation can be gained from this experience, and it has relevance to the present. Selective-service officials had a low opinion of psychiatry, and when war appeared imminent they did not give high priority to psychiatric selection. Most of the incentive for psychiatric screening came from groups within the psychiatric profession, so psychiatrists were in no sense innocent maidens in this affair. Many of the psychiatric recommendations—such as the idea that one psychiatrist be assigned to draft-examining boards for every 50 registrants—were absurd in light of the psychiatric manpower situation. Moreover, the recommendations for psychiatric screening did not show an adequate appreciation of the administrative needs of selective service and the relative priorities given to their goals—of which the major one was manpower procurement. Later in the war, mechanisms were devised which facilitated psychiatric screening, but the responsibility for the failure of screening must reside very largely within the psychiatric profession, which encouraged the entire venture and which made unrealistic claims as to what could be achieved.

In current psychiatric literature, it is impressive to note the many public programs advocated which involve psychiatry but which are unrealistic in terms of manpower, the existing state of psychiatric knowledge, and the organizational and community resources. All too often programs are advocated and encouraged without sufficient attention being given to their feasibility or to their consequences for social and political goals outside the realm of mental health. As psychiatry and public policy increasingly become linked, it is necessary that psychiatric advocates give attention to ideal psychiatric programs not only from a theoretical point of view but also from a practical one.

Post-World War II Developments in Mental Health Policy

World War II not only alerted the country to mental health needs but also provided psychiatry with opportunities to develop programs for psychiatrically disabled soldiers. Although the war brought no breakthroughs in psychiatric knowledge, it did provide individual psychiatrists with broad administrative experience and gave considerable stimulus to attempts to devise new treatment techniques and approaches that were feasible in dealing with relatively large groups of patients. If selective service did little to enhance the reputation of psychiatry, the practical response of psychiatrists in the military to very difficult psychiatric problems was impressive. They showed an openness to new approaches—not always so obvious in psychiatry—and group techniques were used in psychiatry for the first time in any extensive way. Army psychiatrists also experimented with the use of sedation and hypnosis in therapy. Moreover, the psychiatric problems that commonly occurred alerted psychiatrists, more than ever before, to the social aspects of psychiatric care and to the effects of environment on the occurrence of mental illness. By the time the war ended, psychiatrists had gained many friends and a somewhat more receptive response among their medical colleagues.

The publicity given to psychiatric casualties and the awareness of the large manpower loss due to the alleged high prevalence of psychiatric defects in the screened population provided a strong impetus for development of public policy in relation to mental health. The government and informed laymen became aware of the necessity to learn more about the causes of mental illness and the means of preventing it, to assist the individual states in developing their own mental health programs, and to build a satisfactory manpower pool in the mental health area. In 1946 Congress passed the Mental Health Act, which created the National Institute of Mental Health (NIMH). The avowed intent was to have "the traditional public health approach applied to the mental health field." This program did and continues to do much to achieve the goals set for it. One can gain some conception of the growing involvement of the government in mental health simply by comparing the budgets of the NIMH in 1950, 1960, and 1967. From less than 9 million dollars in 1950, it grew to 68 million dollars in 1960 and to 338 million dollars in 1967.

Postwar Psychiatry

The emphasis on private psychiatric care encouraged by psychoanalytic theory and practice did little to facilitate the care of chronic patients in American mental hospitals despite the overall improvement in the psychiatric manpower situation. Most psychiatrists continue to devote themselves to treating patients with mild and moderate problems of living in private therapeutic situations (Hollingshead and Redlich, 1958; Myers and Bean, 1968). Moreover, psychodynamic ideology, which emphasizes analysis of unconscious motivation, has discouraged interest among psychiatrists in more direct and "superficial" techniques of providing support, assurance, and direction.

The tremendous discrepancy between the provision of private and of public services in psychiatry has not existed in most European countries. In England, for example, most of the available and well-trained psychiatric manpower is in the mental hospitals (and increasingly in general hospitals), dealing with severe mental illness of an acute character and with chronic disability. The organization of psychiatric services has, thus, facilitated the development of new programs in hospital and community psychiatry, and English hospitals have been very innovative in this regard (Roberts, 1967). In 1959 Parliament passed the Mental Health Act, which ended the legal designations of mental hospital and mental patient. Any mental patient can be admitted informally to any hospital providing suitable care. Moreover, the Mental Health Act placed emphasis on the development of community care facilities for mental patients and on such additional facilities as hostels, clubs, sheltered workshops, and retraining units. Finally, the act set up stringent criteria for formal certification (commitment) of mental patients, provided checks to protect patients against involuntary care, and set up procedures for regularized reviews of such involuntary admissions.

Although there were significant advances in the United States in manpower development and mental health research following World War II, very little of this gain was transferred to mental hospitals, and direct federal aid to the states for mental health services actually decreased during the Korean War. Although innovations were being developed—most significantly new psychoactive drugs such as tranquilizers—most states had neither the facilities and financial resources nor the personnel to implement new ideas in the mental health field. The Hoover Commission, looking into the entire issue of government reorganization, reported, "Although we believe that the federal government should gradually reduce its grants as the states take up the load for any given health activity, we conclude that the recent reduction in federal support has been too abrupt." (Hoover Commission, 1955, p. 72) The Commission noted that aid to the states had been reduced significantly while research support had been developing. Individual states were becoming acutely aware of their personnel and financial limitations at the same time that a tentative optimistic spirit was emerging in the mental health field because of reports of improved release rates with intensive personal care and drug therapies.

These influences led to Congressional concern, and when the Mental Health Study Act of 1955 was being considered, government officials no longer believed that large custodial institutions could effectively deal with mental illness. At the same time the emphasis on discussion of mental health care in the community was motivated as much by a desire to reduce hospital populations and concomitant costs as by a belief that such measures would have significant therapeutic value. In its deliberations, the Congress gave highest priority to considerations of manpower. The feeling was that already existing therapeutic knowledge could not be applied because of shortages of personnel and facilities. In addition, government officials felt that possible remedial efforts could be increased significantly through the development of psychoactive drugs. In general, however, the experience with new drugs had not progressed to the point where they dominated the thinking of the Congress, and it is likely that the Mental Health Study Act would have been supported in their absence.

The Congress in passing the Mental Health Study Act authorized an appropriation to the Joint Commission on Mental Illness and Health to study and make recommendations concerning various aspects of mental health policy. In 1961 the Commission published its well-known report, *Action for Mental Health,* which argued strongly for an increased program of services and more funds for basic, long-term mental health research. It recommended that expenditures in the mental health field be doubled in 5 years and tripled in 10 years. It argued for new and better recruitment and training programs for mental health workers. It suggested the expansion of treatment programs for acutely ill patients in all facilities including community mental health clinics, general hospitals, and mental hospitals. It argued for the establishment of mental health clinics, suggesting that one would be appropriate for every 50,000 persons in the population. It attacked the large state mental hospitals and suggested that these be converted to smaller, regional, intensive-treatment centers with no more than 1,000 beds. It recommended new programs for the care of chronic patients as well as for aftercare and other rehabilitation services. In short, these were wide-ranging and ambitious demands, and they fell on receptive ears in Washington. Many of these recommendations have since led to action because of abundant funds and moral support from the federal government. The most far-reaching of such legislation is the new program for financing community mental health clinics. This program, is likely to have a profound influence on the distribution of psychiatric services and on the social structure of the mental health professions.

The new direction of mental health policies in the United States, however, did not flow directly from the report of the Joint Commission. *Action for Mental Health* was largely an ideological document, and like poetry it was sufficiently ambiguous to allow various interest groups to read what they wished into it. It is, therefore, not surprising that a vigorous political battle resulted at the federal level between those psychiatrists with a public health viewpoint, who wished to develop completely new precedents for mental patient care, and those psychiatrists more within the traditional medical model, who felt that considerable fed-

eral assistance should be invested in improving the quality of mental hospitals and their capacities to provide adequate treatment to patients.
Those who favored a more radical break with the past system of providing
mental health services through state and federal hospitals were more influential with President John Kennedy, and the final decision was to give
greatest impetus to the community health centers, which were to be developed for the most part independently of the old mental hospital system, although affiliated with it. This was a tremendously important
decision and one which implicitly endorsed the viewpoint that mental
illness is not inherently different from the larger range of psychological
difficulties common in the community. It is perhaps too early to attempt
to evaluate the consequences of this decision, but clearly it has directed
the development of new mental health services toward a particular perspective.

The implementation of many such Joint Commission recommendations required more than the suggestions themselves. First, the American
economy was in an excellent position, and abundant funds were available
for meeting domestic needs. Second, the President himself was very much
committed to the program in mental health and mental retardation, and
in contrast to some other proposed medical care programs, the mental
health program did not involve any obvious group or value cleavages.
Third, psychiatric drugs had changed the climate of mental health care
as well as administrative attitudes, and the value of supporting mental
health services seemed to be more obvious to laymen. Finally, the harmful
consequences of the custodial-hospital environment had been poignantly
demonstrated, and society had become increasingly aware of the unequal
access to good psychiatric treatment for the rich and the poor.

The ideas of the Joint Commission were hardly new. For example,
the Massachusetts State Board of Insanity in 1914 recommended that
"each hospital reach out in the community and be responsible for the
mental health of the district covered by each" and advocated outpatient
departments dealing with aftercare, family care, and mental hygiene.
These departments would take on such functions as working with discharged patients, boarding patients in foster families, and educating the
public to prevent insanity (Grob, 1966, p. 350). What made the report of
the Joint Commission so important was not the uniqueness of its recommendations but rather the receptive climate in which they were introduced. Plausibly any reasonable set of recommendations would have been
acceptable given the timing, circumstances, and mood of the people in
government.

Clearly, from the point of view of public policy, vast changes have
been initiated in the mental health field in just one decade. The flow of
funds for developing preventive and community treatment services puts

the power and initiative of the government behind this "new" concept for providing mental health services. To fully understand the character and extent of these new policies, we must retrace, to some extent, the situation that existed following World War II in state mental hospitals, where most of the nation's mental patients were housed.

The Organization of State Mental Hospitals

The state mental hospitals—where most chronic mental patients are still cared for—were built in the latter part of the nineteenth century and the early part of the twentieth. Many either were developed or were enlarged in response to the crusade of Dorothea Dix; their construction constituted the first attempt in many areas of the country to provide any attention at all for persons of limited resources who were mentally ill. But, for the most part, these hospitals provided inferior custodial care to a growing number of patients. Although hospital admissions increased, in part because of conditions associated with the changing character of American society, such as industrialization, concentration of the population, and large waves of immigration, mental health policy was typified by a considerable feeling of hopelessness about constructive action, and mental health was given low priority relative to other social needs. This situation persisted well into the present century despite several attempts to humanize the mental hospital.

The major humanizing influence on mental hospitals earlier in the twentieth century was the Mental Hygiene Movement. Begun by Clifford Beers, a former mental patient who exposed the dehumanizing aspects of mental patient care, this movement encouraged a new, humanistic ideology which stimulated some improvement in hospital conditions and public concern for the mentally ill. It did little, however, to retard the pattern of providing for the mentally ill in large and impersonal public institutions. Despite the efforts and concern of many reformers, mental hospitals maintained a custodial attitude reinforced by meager allowances for the care of psychiatric patients, limited professional staff, and dependence on untrained and unskilled manpower.

One of the most important innovations in mental patient care has been the use of psychoactive drugs, first introduced in the middle 1950s. Although these drugs do not cure patients, they do much to reduce their most disturbing symptoms; they thereby facilitate the control of mental patients and the ability of hospital personnel to work with them. The use of drugs gave the staff greater confidence in its own efficacy and helped dispel the feeling of hopelessness and apathy that had captured the mental hospital. All these conditions gave impetus to administrative changes such as eliminating constraints, minimizing security arrangements, and encouraging early release. From the point of view of the patient's relatives and the community in general, patients under drug treatment were more tractable and cooperative, and thus community receptivity to mental patients returning to the community increased. Finally, the feeling of hope and efficacy felt by the hospital staff was communicated to patients and the community generally and gave both renewed confidence in the ability of patients to cope with difficulties outside the hospital.

Evidence supports the contention that changes in patient retention and release patterns following the introduction of psychoactive drugs were as much the result of administrative changes in mental hospitals as they were the consequence of the drugs themselves. Some studies in English hospitals that introduced new administrative policies prior to the introduction of psychoactive drugs show that new patterns of release were observable prior to drug introduction, and they suggest that the tremendous change that took place is largely due to alterations in administrative policies. Whatever the specific utility of the psychoactive drugs, the development of this new technology provided a climate of opinion and confidence in which it became possible to change important policies relating to patient handling and release. Whether directly or indirectly, drugs helped bring about a revolution in psychiatric care.

Statistics on patients resident in mental hospitals reflect the vast changes that took place. At the end of 1955, 558,922 patients were residents in mental hospitals, but the following years show a considerable decrease in this figure. Although the number of admissions to mental hospitals was substantially rising between 1955 and 1964, by the latter year only 490,754 patients were residents in mental hospitals (Clausen, 1961). Moreover, the new attitudes that developed during the period in which the psychoactive drugs were introduced led to vast changes of programs, procedures, and attitudes toward patients.

Despite many of these favorable changes, the mental hospitals continue to be plagued by many of the problems and conditions which preceded these administrative and therapeutic advances. Most are still characterized by large size and limited staff; managing such institutions demands organizational routines which interfere with an individualized approach to the patient. For the most part, patients have limited contact with professional staff on an individual level, and their care and treatment do not appear to be based on any overall rational plan. Much time in the mental hospital is spent doing nothing to enhance the patient's understanding of his problems or to develop new skills and techniques which would allow him to cope successfully with the problems and difficulties that led to his hospitalization. Despite the obvious need to improve the quality of these hospitals and their staffing patterns, officials of the federal government decided to make only limited resources available for hospital improvement in contrast to those made available for community care.

New Programs of Community Care

Many of the added activities which have been supported by public investment in the mental health field have been in the area of community care. The community care ideology developed from the growing realization that the mental hospital as it existed did much to isolate the patient from his community, to undermine his motivation to return, to retard his skills, and, in general, to induce a level of disability above and beyond that resulting from the patient's condition. As noted earlier, the report of the Joint Commission attacked the large mental hospitals and advocated their abolition. In contrast, the Commission supported smaller mental hospitals providing intensive care, treatment units in general hospitals, mental health centers, and the like. These facilities were close to the patient's home and kept him in touch with his family and the community. Thus, the new emphasis is on outpatient care and short periods of hospitalization when necessary. Moreover, new alternatives were urged which fell somewhere between the total separation characterized by the mental hospital in isolation from the community and outpatient care. If some form of institutional care is necessary, less radical alternatives than full-time hospitalization can be implemented—day hospitals, night hospitals, halfway houses, hostels, and so on. Moreover, an understanding of the importance of maintaining patients' skills and sense of activity led to added emphasis on vocational services, sheltered workshops, continuing employment while the patient was in the hospital, and the like. Finally, great emphasis has been given to the idea that patients should be kept in their home surroundings and that the necessary services should be provided to them and their families so that they can cope with the problems that arise.

Ideologies develop more rapidly than patterns of care, and while it was not terribly difficult, speaking relatively, to change hospital policies concerning admission and retention, there are additional obstacles in providing a system of community services that can support and buttress new hospital policies so as to ensure maximum benefits for patients. Thus, while the ideology is coherent, the services provided to patients in the community are sporadic and fragmentary, and frequently the burden that had been the hospital's has been shifted to the family. Yet in most parts of the country no system of services aids the family in meeting crises or in dealing with the patient and the problems of his care effectively. Indeed, many new developments are now being directed toward these ends.

This section of our discussion has been mainly descriptive, and although we have reviewed some of the historical elements in the evolution of mental health policy in relation to mental health services, we have not examined the issues and dilemmas that various program alternatives raise. In Chapter 6 we shall turn to such issues and explore in detail the consequences—both intended and unintended—of pursuing particular policies. Before doing this, however, we must explore in greater detail the community processes leading to definitions of mental illness.

Chapter 5

THE RECOGNITION OF MENTAL DISORDERS

The extent to which mental illness is seen to exist depends on the perspectives taken and the criteria used to identify its presence. In this area it is not too difficult to play a numbers game which either maximizes or minimizes the amount of alleged mental illness by changing the criteria used. If mental illness is viewed as the presence of a clearly established disabling condition, then the estimate of its occurrence is conservative. However, if mental illness is also defined as the presence of psychosomatic conditions, anxiety, or any of a wide variety of problems in living, then we can characterize a large proportion of the population as having some form of mental illness.

A study of midtown Manhattan (Srole *et al.*, 1962) given much attention estimated that approximately one-quarter of the more than 1,600 respondents between 20 and 59 years of age who were surveyed were impaired. It evaluated only 18.5 per cent of the total respondent group as being healthy. Other studies have made similar observations (see Leighton *et al.*, 1963). In a study of the prevalence of mental disorders in Kalamazoo County, Michigan (Manis *et al.*, 1964), in which various data comparable to those collected in midtown Manhattan were obtained, the investigators demonstrated that the rates of mental illness in midtown

Manhattan were not very different from those in the community they studied but that they were inflated by the different criteria used.

> Our interpretation is that the differences in reported rates of untreated illness arise *primarily* from lack of agreement, stated or implicit, in the criteria used to establish the cutting-point between the sick and the well. The criterion used in the Kalamazoo community study appears to identify only the extremely ill and to under estimate total prevalence. The Baltimore procedures seem to focus on a more broadly conceived spectrum to mental illness, though they, too, admit some underestimation. The rates reported for Midtown Manhattan are apparently the consequence of a very inclusive conception of mental illness. (p. 89)

R. J. Plunkett and J. E. Gordon (1960), reviewing prevalence studies undertaken prior to 1960, note that percentages of the population found to be mentally ill range from less than 2 per cent to as much as 33 per cent (pp. 62–68). With the inadequacies of the measures used in various surveys and field studies, it seems reasonable to use such measures primarily for assessing relative differences among population groups rather than to treat the absolute levels of disorder reported as meaningful assessments (Davis, 1965).

A paper by Bruce and Barbara Dohrenwend (1968) illustrates clearly the unreliability of various absolute estimates of psychiatric illness. In reviewing 25 studies of untreated cases of psychological disorder, they found that prevalence rates varied from less than 1 per cent to over 60 per cent of the population. And comparing epidemiological studies carried out in 1950 or earlier with those done after 1950, they found widely varying rates of pathology. The median rate in the studies after 1950 was more than seven times the one reported for the earlier studies. Since it is inconceivable that population rates have changed so radically, it is clear that these estimates are very unstable.

By considering limited categories of mental illness one can increase the possibility of making some reasonable estimate of morbidity. Investigators, using relatively limited concepts of schizophrenia, in different countries, agree that the prevalence of active cases varies from approximately one-quarter to one-half of 1 per cent of the population (Wing, 1967; L. Wing *et al.,* 1967). As the concept expands, of course, the prevalence rate increases. From the point of view of public policy, questions concerning the prevalence of mental illness must be linked to decisions concerning the appropriate range of facilities that should be provided. Once we have some conception of which conditions it is reasonable to treat, we can estimate the extent of the problem we have to deal with.

Planning for psychiatric services is not vastly different from planning for general medical services. If we wish to improve the facilities available for dealing with a variety of diseases for which medical care is important, and we thus require estimates of community needs, we do not survey the population to determine the prevalence of the common cold. Similarly, in deciding the magnitude of psychiatric need in the population, we must not confuse the psychiatric conditions causing profound distress and disability with the prevalence of mild difficulties and mild psychophysiological complaints. I do not wish to imply that help should not be available to those who have such difficulties, but, just as we do not confuse the common cold with heart disease, so should we not confuse psychoses or severe neurotic problems with common complaints. Estimates of the proportion of the population who are neurotic range from as little as less than five in 100 to very large proportions of the total population. Some psychiatrists who advocate a dynamic perspective go as far as to argue that everyone in the population is neurotic and that we all could benefit from a better understanding of our intrapsychic needs and repressed desires. While such a point of view may have some value as a philosophical statement, the absence of criteria for discriminating among those more or less needy makes such positions irrelevant in the development of public policy.

In considering the issue of need we should not be confused by the distinction between neurosis and psychosis. Although these terms, as they are used in a general sense, connote gradations of severity of illness, specific neurotic conditions cause profound distress, are incapacitating, and are amenable to effective care. It is irresponsible to confuse such conditions with those that do not cause severe discomfort, do not prevent persons from performing their social roles reasonably, and do not respond in any clear way to psychiatric intervention. While some neurotic conditions require intensive and sophisticated care and are sufficiently serious to require a coherent public approach, other conditions similarly labeled are trivial and are unworthy of serious concern until the more profound and disabling conditions are adequately cared for. Thus, it is extremely difficult to make adequate estimates of the need for help in the general area of the neuroses until the designation itself is more carefully defined, and until the criteria for the recognition of the serious conditions within this realm are more specifically elaborated.

Except in the case of blatant psychiatric conditions demanding public intervention, it is very difficult to estimate the need for facilities since the need for care is ordinarily not defined by professional criteria but rather by members of the community who decide whether to seek psychiatric care for themselves or others and under what conditions. Since definition and intervention occur within the community, we should understand the social and personal processes through which persons come to see themselves or others as suffering from a psychiatric condition and how they come to the attention of psychiatric facilities.

Mental Illness, Illness Behavior, and the
Help-Seeking Process

There have been several attempts to develop social-psychological models which provide a clear conception of how people come to the realization that they are ill and how they decide that some form of action is necessary. J. M. Rosenstock (1960) suggests that preventive health behavior is determined by the extent to which a person sees a problem as having both serious consequences and a high probability of occurrence. He further believes that behavior emerges from conflicting goals and motives and that action follows from those motives which are most salient and those goals which are perceived as most valuable. I. Zola (1964), approaching the problem from another perspective, attempts to delineate five "triggers" in the timing of patients' decisions to seek medical care. In the first pattern, interpersonal crisis, the situation calls attention to the symptoms and causes the patient to dwell on them. In the second situation, social interference, the symptoms are the same, but they threaten a valued social activity. The third, sanctioning, involves others telling the patient to seek care. The fourth is the patient's perception of the symptoms as a threat; and the fifth is the patient's knowledge of the nature and quality of the symptoms. The last trigger involves recognition of the similarity of the symptoms to previous ones or to those of friends. Zola reports his impression that these triggers have different degrees of importance in varying social strata and ethnic groups. He suggests that interpersonal crisis and social interference are prevalent causes among Italians, while sanctioning is the predominant Irish pattern. The Anglo-Saxon group responds most to recognition of the nature and quality of their symptoms.

The range of factors discussed in relation to the various responses to symptoms, fall into ten sets (Mechanic, 1968).

1. The visibility, recognizability, or perceptual salience of deviant signs and symptoms.
2. The extent to which the person perceives the symptoms as serious (that is, the person's estimate of the present and future probabilities of danger).
3. The extent to which symptoms disrupt family, work, and other social activities.
4. The frequency of the appearance of deviant signs or symptoms, or their persistence.
5. The tolerance threshold of those who are exposed to and evaluate the deviant signs and symptoms.
6. The information available to, the knowledge of, and the cultural assumptions and understandings of the evaluator.

7. The degree to which autistic psychological processes (i.e., perceptual processes that distort reality) are present.
8. The presence of needs that conflict with the recognition of illness or the assumption of the sick role.
9. The possibility that competing interpretations can be assigned to the symptoms once they are recognized.
10. The availability of treatment resources, their physical proximity, and the psychological and monetary costs of taking action (included are not only physical distance and costs of time, money, and effort, but also such costs as stigmatization, resulting social distance, and feelings of humiliation resulting from a particular illness definition).

It may appear curious that I should attempt to group together factors affecting the recognition and the definition of both psychiatric and non-psychiatric disorders since we know that mental patients are often brought into care through different pathways from those followed by people who suffer from general medical conditions. For example, a large proportion of psychotics among the lower class are first recognized as mentally ill when their bizarre behavior becomes visible to community authorities; such persons are frequently brought to a psychiatric facility by police personnel. Similarly, alcoholics and drug addicts brought into treatment often come through official routes such as the courts, the police, or community social agencies. Although we must realize that different kinds of patients come into care through different pathways, we should also note that the general social processes leading to the recognition and the identification of general medical conditions and those leading to the recognition of psychiatric problems are very similar. All illness is defined because the person directly concerned or others become aware that some deviation from a normal state has taken place. The community may have more tolerance for a person with a broken leg or for one who is shy and withdrawn than for the alcoholic who disturbs others or the schizophrenic who verbalizes thoughts no one can understand. But the differences in defining a person with a broken leg and in defining a disruptive alcoholic stem not from different social processes but rather from the manner in which these conditions become manifest and from their effect on social life, social activities, and social values. If you are aware that a member of your living group has active tuberculosis, and he refuses to seek treatment—thus exposing you to his disease—you might choose to use official agencies to ensure that he is removed from contact with you and does not threaten the public safety. In short, what makes ordinary medical conditions different from psychiatric ones, from the public's standpoint, are the various ways in which psychiatric disorders differ in terms of the ten dimensions already noted.

We have no way of predicting the specific response to any condition. The definitions of normality by which deviation is judged vary among medical practitioners as well as among lay persons, especially in the area of psychiatric disorders. More frequently than not individuals come to view themselves as ill on the basis of their own standards of functioning as well as on their previous knowledge and experience, and when marked deviations are apparent they tend to seek medical confirmation. On other occasions the individual does not recognize himself as sick but comes to accept this definition when some other person defines him as ill (as occurs, for example, in the case of a person who is informed that he has hypertension or tuberculosis, although he may not actually recognize that he is ill). On some occasions, others define a person as sick, but he vigorously resists this definition. Since the definition that one is mentally ill involves a considerable change in one's self-identity and since the effects of treatment are often perceived as uncertain or harmful, it is not surprising that persons designated as mentally ill are resistant to being defined in this way. But even this difference can be exaggerated, and the overlap in this respect between psychiatric and nonpsychiatric conditions is considerable.

The manner in which deviant feelings or behavior becomes evident may have varying disruptive effects on social life and may be associated with more or less stigma. While some mentally ill persons withdraw from social interaction and cause no disruption in the community, others engage in visible, bizarre behavior which is threatening and frightening to others. In general, the person whose symptoms are not disruptive is not so readily defined since the public's conceptions of health and mental illness tend to be sharply polarized. Because the behavior of mentally ill persons is viewed as markedly different from that of normal individuals, the public frequently stigmatizes persons so defined. Thus psychiatric conditions, as opposed to nonpsychiatric ones, tend to be more disruptive and associated with greater stigma, but we should again note that this difference is a quantitative rather than a qualitative one. We do not need to consider the social processes underlying the definitions of psychiatric and nonpsychiatric conditions separately, as long as we give attention to such factors as social disruption, stigma, and resistance to accepting a definition of illness.

The ten categories discussed previously pertain equally to situations in which an individual defines himself as ill and to those in which others in association with him come to regard him as "sick." For example, let us consider how these categories apply to a man suffering from a self-defined depressive condition and to an alcoholic defined as a problem by the community. The recognition of a depressive illness may follow a period during which a person experiences feelings of sadness and emptiness more profound than usual, difficulty getting going, loss of interest in life, sluggishness, and the like. But depression is a fairly common symptom, and the person must recognize that this depression is more serious than the bouts he may have previously experienced. This recognition, in turn, depends on the extent to which his symptoms disrupt his activities, the persistence of the depression and associated symptoms, the person's tolerance for psychological pain, and so on. More specifically, a self-definition of illness may depend on whether the depressed state is sufficiently profound so that the person cannot get himself out of bed, get to work, or take on his usual responsibilities and activities, and on whether the symptoms are persistent or fluctuating. Moreover, the person may be able to assign competing definitions to his symptoms. For example, if he has suffered some adversity, such as the death or injury of a loved one or a personal defeat in his work or family life, he may define his feeling state and condition as a temporary response to a frustrating and unhappy situation. But should these symptoms occur independently of adversity, the person is likely to view the problem as coming from within himself.

These categories can be applied equally well to definitions of alcoholics, schizophrenics, or other persons often designated by the community as mentally ill. The community is more likely to define an individual as an alcoholic when his drinking is visible rather than private and when his drinking pattern extends beyond that ordinarily thought of as conventional. The definition of and response of others to such excessive drinking depend on how serious the person's drinking is regarded; the extent to which his drinking disrupts work, family, and other community activities; the frequency with which he becomes drunk; and so on. For example, if the person's drinking leads to work absenteeism, conflict within the family, and embarrassing family situations, he is more likely to be defined as a problem than he is if he drinks himself to sleep at night and does not disrupt family life or fail to meet social obligations. Similarly, persons in the community may have more or less tolerance for drinking and drunkenness. They may not take note of a happy drunk but may react punitively to a drunk involved in fights or driving a motor vehicle. It is not my intent to go into each of these matters in any detail. The point is that from a conceptual view, we do not need to develop separate categories for the factors underlying the social definition of illness made by the person himself and for those underlying the definitions made by others. (For a more complete discussion, see Mechanic (1968).)

Various investigators have studied the conditions under which a particular set of symptoms are viewed from a psychiatric frame of reference or from some other perspective. Charles Kadushin (1958), in interviews with 110 persons using a psychiatric clinic, attempted to ascertain how they decided to undertake psychotherapy. He found that such a decision is a five-step process: (1) the person must decide that he has a problem and that it is an emotional one; (2) he must decide whether to discuss the problem with his relatives and friends; (3) he must at some point decide whether he is adequately dealing with the problem and whether to seek professional help; (4) if he chooses to seek professional help, he must choose an appropriate profession to seek help from; and (5) he must select a particular practitioner. In his clinic sample Kadushin found four characteristic ways of recognizing a problem: being told by others, experiencing painful physical symptoms, being unhappily married, and feeling unhappy in general. In a further analysis of social distance between client and professional, Kadushin (1962) found that stable interaction is most likely when there is little social distance between role partners, so that professionals who are socially close to clients are likely to be consulted. He further points out that the patient's lack of familiarity with the psychotherapist's role can also be a problem. Kadushin (1966) feels that some of these problems are alleviated through the presence of a subculture of friends and supporters of psychotherapy, and he argues that knowing others who have had psychiatric treatment, being told by one's friends to go to a psychiatrist, having one's problems noticed by others, and reading works on psychoanalysis are characteristics of those belonging to this subculture (1962, p. 530). Kadushin's analysis pertains only to some kinds of psychiatric patients; the process of defining oneself as mentally ill may vary very substantially from one type of psychiatric condition to another.

If the subculture Kadushin describes exists and makes persons more receptive to particular treatment contexts, then the use of some psychiatric services may depend not so much on the seriousness of the person's condition as on whether he is a member of the informal subculture. A study by T. Scheff (1966b) of users and nonusers of a student psychiatric clinic sheds some light on this issue. Scheff compared a sample of student applicants for psychiatric help with a random sample of the population that had free access to this psychiatric clinic. The items on the questionnaires administered to both groups were almost identical; they were largely concerned with the problems of students and had been developed from studying the problems of previous students who had applied for psychiatric help. Scheff found that the number of problems students reported was strongly related to application for psychiatric care: 59 per cent of the clinic applicants had ten or more problems, while only 35 per cent of the nonusers had a similar number. The most striking aspect of this result, however, is the very extensive overlap between clinic applicants and the random sample in respect to the problem inventory. An equally impressive result is that religion and religious participation were more effective predictors of clinic applications than was the number of problems students had. Overall, Scheff found that the clinic sample had an overrepresentation of persons with similar social backgrounds and similar social activities.

L. Linn (1967), in another study of the same psychiatric clinic, provides further evidence in support of the general idea developed by Kadushin. In comparing clinic applicants with a random sample to whom clinic services were available, he argued that there would be an overrepresentation of applicants from the group of students who were less integrated into traditional social institutions, who were more likely to identify with other students who were cosmopolitan, who were more likely to report that they had friends with socioemotional problems, and who discussed such problems with others. Linn presents considerable evidence in support of these ideas. He found an overrepresentation of clinic applicants among those who reported that their friends were interested in psychology, were concerned about meaning in life, and were sensitive and introspective; he found an underrepresentation of those who reported that they liked football games, were religious, and had friends who were usually well dressed (see also Bart, 1968).

Although knowledge of, interest in, and receptivity to psychiatry as reflected in the social-circle concept of Kadushin are important, other factors also differentiate users and nonusers of psychiatric facilities. In an important study involving the use of child-guidance facilities, the investigators found that seeking care for children with specific problems was related to a variety of factors including socioeconomic status, parental age, and size and composition of the family (Shepherd *et al.*, 1966). Also involved in the process of help-seeking were the mental health of mothers and other parental responses. In contrast to mothers who did not have children in the clinic, mothers of clinic children were more likely to be anxious, depressed, and easily upset by stress; they felt less able to cope with their children; and they were more likely to discuss their problems and to seek advice.

Community Definitions of Mental Illness

Many psychiatric conditions are defined not by the person himself but by others in the community who note the person's bizarre behavior or failure to meet expected standards. Such labeling of a particular person as mentally ill depends on the various contingencies discussed earlier. In addition to the influences of different personal and social factors, the character of the symptoms themselves exert a considerable effect on whether a person is defined as mentally ill. Although there are vast differences in willingness to tolerate bizarre and difficult behavior, for example, few relatives are willing to house a patient who is suicidal, homicidal, incontinent, hallucinatory, delusional, or disoriented (Angrist *et al.,* 1963). In short, if the patient is sufficiently bizarre and disruptive, the probability is extremely high that he will come into care. Social definitions of illness are relevant because many serious illnesses do not develop in a particularly striking way. The ambiguity surrounding the occurrence and the severity of illness makes sociological variables important.

Although the public's conception of mental illness has been changing to some extent, there is considerable reluctance to define a relative or friend as mentally ill and a strong tendency to normalize and to deny symptoms that become apparent. Indeed, as we mentioned earlier, the public often visualizes mental illnesses as extreme states of disorganized behavior and as a very sharp break from usual or familiar patterns. Lesser psychiatric difficulties are often viewed as physical conditions or as indications of normal variabilities in personality. When the person's symptoms are accompanied by physical indications, he is often urged to seek medical help. But should his difficult behavior be inconsistent with a physical interpretation, then it is often attributed to stubbornness or to moral defects rather than to illness.

J. Clausen, M. R. Yarrow (1955), and their colleagues describe five trends that characterize the process through which wives of psychiatric patients attempt to cope with their husbands' mental illness and increasingly difficult behavior. (1) The wife's first recognition of a problem depends on the accumulation of behavior which is not readily understandable or acceptable to her; (2) this recognition forces her to examine the situation and to adjust her expectations for herself and for her husband to account for his deviant response; (3) the wife's interpretation of the problem shifts back and forth from seeing the situation as normal on one occasion to seeing it as abnormal on another; (4) she tends to make continuous adaptations to the behavior of her spouse, waiting for additional cues that either confirm her definition or lead to a new one. She mobilizes strong defenses against her husband's deviant behavior; and (5) finally, she reaches the point at which she can no longer sustain a definition of normality and cope with her husband's behavior. Yarrow (1955) observes the following tendencies.

> The most obvious form of defense in the wife's response is the tendency to *normalize* the husband's neurotic and psychotic symptoms. His behavior is explained, justified, or made acceptable by seeing it also in herself or by assuring herself that the particular behavior occurs again and again among persons who are not ill. . . . When behavior cannot be normalized, it can be made to seem less severe or less important in a total picture than an outsider might see it. By finding some grounds for the behavior or something explainable about it, the wife achieves at least momentary

attenuation of the seriousness of it. By *balancing* acceptable with unacceptable behavior or "strange" with "normal" behavior, some wives can conclude that the husband is not seriously disturbed. Defense sometimes amounts to a thoroughgoing *denial*. This takes the form of denying that the behavior perceived can be interpreted in an emotional or psychiatric framework. (pp. 22–23)

The strong tendency of relatives and the community to normalize difficult patterns of behavior until they can no longer be tolerated has relevance for public policy since it encourages long delays in seeking treatment. Awareness of such common tendencies has encouraged public health psychiatrists to support efforts toward public education. Many argue that it is first necessary to educate the public to recognize the appearance of mental illness in its earliest manifestations and to view seeking aid for these problems as appropriate. Moreover, efforts have been made in recent years to provide community facilities other than mental hospitals that are especially prepared to deal with these problems.

This failure to recognize mental illness and at times the blatant denial of it are not such simple or clear-cut issues as they may seem. Very large costs are involved in recognizing oneself, one's spouse, or one's child as mentally ill. The definitional act itself often involves major changes in the structure of interaction in the family; indeed, the recognition that a member of the family is mentally ill requires a major reorganization of the family itself. Moreover, once the definition is made and action is taken, the act is in many ways irreversible. The meanings that members of the family assign to one another have been changed, the stigma of mental illness cannot be completely reversed, and, perhaps what is most important of all, psychiatric assistance may not make any significant difference in restoring "normality" to the situation.

From a policy perspective there is at least one other consideration. Many of these crises may be transient ones, and the usual patterns of family living may be restored at less cost without outside assistance. The studies and observations on normalization are extremely biased ones. They concentrate on situations in which *the normalization process has failed and has led to further problems.* Although we have no adequate data to make an absolute judgment these situations may constitute a rather small percentage of the total population of cases in which bizarre behavior occurs and normalization takes place. There are reasonable indications that a large proportion of bizarre psychiatric symptoms are, in fact, transitory.

If we could successfully identify family crises early, it is not at all clear that it would be advantageous for individuals or society to pursue a policy of placing these problems in a psychiatric or mental health perspective. The act of defining a person's behavior as indicative of a psychiatric condition may undermine his limited self-confidence and efforts at continuing to cope in work and family life, and it may encourage a stance of dependency which leads to further disability and the acceptance of illness. Thus, the major challenge faced by new programs is to provide sustenance and help to those who are going through difficult crises without defining and structuring their problems so as to increase the probability of disability.

To some extent, the experience of the military in the psychiatric area illustrates the consequences of various alternatives. Evaluations of the use of psychotherapy in dealing with neuropsychiatric casualties indicate that the manner of providing care has a bearing on the effectiveness of the soldier. A. J. Glass (1953) reports that when psychiatric casualties were evacuated to mental health facilities during the North African and Sicilian campaigns in World War II few soldiers were salvaged for combat duty. The psychiatrist, prior to the development of new military mental health policies, usually assumed that the patient was ill and "sought to uncover basic emotional conflicts or attempted to relate current behavior and symptoms with past personality patterns." (p. 288) This administrative policy seemingly provided patients with rational reasons for their combat failures. Both the patient and the therapist were often readily convinced that the limit of combat endurance had been reached. In contrast, when subsequently psychiatrists treated soldiers in the combat zone by such interpersonal devices as suggestion and influence, a much higher percentage of men returned to combat. Glass (1957) argues that neuropsychiatric illness is often the result of an attempt to adapt to or withdraw from dangerous combat circumstances.

> It should be recognized that both symptoms and behavioral abnormalities represent a meaningful effort at adaptation under stress. Inability to cope with threatening or dangerous situations evokes substitute behavior of an evasive or regressive pattern in an effort to reach some satisfactory compromise solution for both internal needs and external demands. Even in the bizarre types of combat psychiatric breakdown, such as mutism or uncontrolled panic flight, one can discern primitive attempts to withdraw or escape from a terrorizing environment. Less severe abnormalities, such as hysterical paralysis, self-inflicted wounds, and AWOL from battle, more readily portray their purposeful nature. In the more mild forms of combat fatigue, characterized by tremulousness, tearfulness and verbal surrender, a childish dependent adaptation is quite evident. The form or type of psychological noneffective behavior displayed in combat is not determined so much by individual personality characteristics as it is dictated either by the practical circumstances of the battle situation or by group (including medical) acceptance of such symptoms or behavior. (pp. 194–95)

We can make a rough assessment of the scope and importance of social definitions in determining morbidity by evaluating the effects of changing psychiatric policies in the military. Despite the shifts in military psychiatric policy from before World War II to after the Korean War, one finds an impressive consistency in the rates of admission to hospitals for armed forces personnel. This consistency suggests that changes in policy had little effect on the occurrence of psychoses requiring hospital care. The invulnerability of rates of psychosis to changing public policies is also supported by the facts that such rates are approximately the same in wartime and in peacetime and that they did not differ appreciably in the two wars under consideration. Moreover, additional evidence shows that extreme combat conditions or exposure to bombing attacks does not have any apparent effect on the rate of occurrence of psychotic conditions (Group for the Advancement of Psychiatry, 1960, pp. 290–91; Glass, 1957; also see the discussion of the influence of stress in Chapter 3).

In contrast, the rates of admission for psychoneurotic conditions fluctuate widely. Among army active-duty personnel they are considerably higher in wartime than they are in peacetime, and they were also considerably higher in World War II than they were in the Korean War. As we noted earlier, the conflicting conceptions of psychoneurosis and the lack of reliability in its diagnosis allow such rates to be easily manipulated. In all overseas theaters in World War II, approximately 23 per cent of all evacuations were due to psychiatric causes; in Japan and Korea from September 1950 to May 1951, the comparable figure was only 6 per cent. In short, military psychiatric policies appear to have had considerable influence on the rate of defined neurotic conditions.

Good evidence suggests that the much lower proportion of evacuations for psychiatric reasons in the Korean War resulted from more than the manipulation of the definition of psychoneurosis. During the Korean War the Army developed a preventive program to retain manpower and to cut down the level of neuropsychiatric casualties. The core of the new program was to provide brief supportive treatment in the combat zone and to avoid a hospital atmosphere or one conducive to adopting a patient role. Studies of such neuropsychiatric cases returned to duty show that their performance was comparable to that of other returnees hospitalized for disease or injury, or excused for administrative reasons (Group for the Advancement of Psychiatry, 1960, pp. 291–92). The Navy has had experience similar to that of the Army. In the Korean War marines were provided supportive treatment close to the front; few were evacuated, and psychiatric casualty rates were one-tenth of those in World War II (Group for the Advancement of Psychiatry, 1960, p. 294).

Such programs of administrative support and therapy based on viewing the soldier's difficulties as being within the normal range under stress do not necessarily cure psychiatric problems, but they do ensure more effective behavior. As we will argue later, few forms of therapy presently available are curative in a meaningful sense. From the perspective of the military, the psychiatric policies pursued during the Korean War were less costly and more useful in promoting effective behavior than were those used in previous wars.

The military situation also sheds light on another matter discussed in Chapter 3 which must be held in mind throughout the entire discussion. Rates of psychoses show little responsiveness to changing conditions and administrative policies, and this suggests, although it cannot be proved, that such conditions are not part of the same continuum as psychoneurotic conditions, which appear to fluctuate widely under varying stress conditions. If we can apply the military experience to other contexts, then mental health policy in relation to chronic mental conditions of a psychotic nature must be formulated on the basis of different considerations from those given to psychoneurotic conditions and other problems of living.

Chapter 6

CENTRAL PERSPECTIVES
IN FORMULATING
MENTAL HEALTH POLICIES

In considering various alternatives for government participation in the mental health area, we immediately recognize several issues and difficulties. This section of the book is devoted to consideration of some important issues relevant to the social functioning of patients within the community.

Criteria for Measuring the Effects of Alternative
Mental Health Programs

Historically, the mental health field has been no stranger to the numbers game in which indices of cure and rehabilitation have been bandied around for administrative and propaganda purposes (Deutsch, 1949). In part, the discouragement and disillusionment of mental health workers in the early twentieth century were caused by the discreditation of phony cure rates, which had become so common among administrators in the preceding period. Past experience suggests that an intelligent assessment of the effects of varying mental health policies must be based on more than admission and release statistics, which are easily manipulated by administrators for their own purposes; they must be based on clinical and social indicators that characterize the outcomes for patients and the community in very specific terms.

The effects of varying mental health policies can be characterized and evaluated in at least three ways: (1) We can measure the subjective response of patients to various kinds of policies, e.g., whether they feel they have been helped, whether they feel they have fewer symptoms and are more able to cope; (2) we can attempt to measure their performance and the quality of their lives after exposure to varying public policies; or (3) we can attempt to assess the consequences of various policies in terms of economic and administrative costs, i.e., does one policy lead to an equivalent outcome at less cost than another does. All these forms of evaluation are important and compatible.

In recent years the most striking change in mental health policy has been in the use of psychiatric hospitalization. Many patients who would have been retained in mental hospitals in the past now return to the community after a relatively short period. Most patients leave the hospital within a year, and the average stay is no more than a few months. In short, if the quality of mental-patient rehabilitation is to be measured by the ability to remain in the community or the ability to return to it, the consequences of new mental health policies have been profound.

The perceived importance of keeping the patient in the community rather than in the hospital is evident from the report of the Joint Commission on Mental Illness and Health (1961) and the legislation that has followed. The report made the following contentions.

> The objective of modern treatment of persons with major mental illness is to enable the patient to maintain himself in the community in a normal manner. To do so, it is necessary (1) to save the patient from the debilitating effects of institutionalism as much as possible, (2) if the patient requires hospitalization, to return him to home and community life as soon as possible, and (3) thereafter to maintain him in the community as long as possible. Therefore, aftercare and rehabilitation are essential parts of all service to mental patients, and the various methods of achieving rehabilitation should be integrated in all forms of services, among them day hospitals, night hospitals, aftercare clinics, public health nursing services, foster family care, convalescent nursing homes, rehabilitation centers, work services, and ex-patient groups. We recommend that demonstration programs for day and night hospitals and the more flexible use of mental hospital facilities, in the treatment of both the acute and chronic patient, be encouraged and augmented through institutional, program, and project grants. (p. xvii)

Returning the patient to the community, in itself, is no panacea if the quality of the patient's life and functioning cannot be improved. With the great emphasis in the American value system on effective performance and carrying one's own weight, it is not surprising that some persons view residence in the community as a good in itself, independent of the quality of the patient's life. But this poses the issue too simply. If the patient is sufficiently aberrant and disturbed, his residence in the community may cause innumerable difficulties for his family and others and may result in a general outcome far inferior to good institutional care. Therefore, we must understand more thoroughly what happens to the mental patient outside the hospital—the extent to which difficulties occur and how they are handled. Intelligent planning of community services depends on a firm understanding of the true consequences of various policies. Unfortunately, informative data in this area are most difficult to obtain.

Thus far the most impressive study promoting an informed public policy comes from an experimental investigation on the prevention of hospitalization (Pasamanick *et al.,* 1967). The major intent of the study was to determine the relative value of hospital versus home treatment for schizophrenic patients under varying circumstances. The investigators randomized 152 schizophrenic patients referred to a state hospital into three groups: (1) a drug home-care group, (2) a placebo home-care group, and (3) a hospital control group. Patients treated at home were visited regularly by public health nurses and were seen less frequently by a staff psychologist, a social worker, and a psychiatrist for evaluation purposes. The study compared hospital treatment and home-care treatment by public health nurses and also compared home-care patients receiving drugs and those not receiving drugs.

Patients were involved in the study from 6 to 30 months. The investigators found that over 77 per cent of the drug home-care patients remained continuously at home in contrast to 34 per cent of those receiving placebos. They estimated, using the hospital control group as a base, that the 57 home patients receiving drugs saved over 4,800 days of hospitalization and that the 41 patients in the placebo group saved over 1,150 inpatient days. They also observed that members of the control group treated in the hospital required rehospitalization more frequently after they returned to the community than did the patients who were treated at home on drugs from the very start. Just on the basis of economic policy these findings are important. The authors came to the following conclusion.

> This carefully designed experimental study confirmed our original hypothesis that home care for schizophrenic patients is *feasible,* that the combination of drug therapy and public health nurses' home visitations is *effective* in preventing hospitalization, and that home care is at least as good a method of treatment as hospitalization by any or all criteria, and probably superior by most. (p. ix)

If one accepts the indicators used by the investigators as adequate criteria for measuring rehabilitation, the results are impressive, and, thus, the adequacy of the indicators used requires careful scrutiny. One aspect of the study raises some question as to whether remaining at home is an adequate measure of rehabilitation. The investigators selected patients for the study when they were referred to the state hospital for treatment. The relatives of the patients randomly selected for home treatment were informed that hospital treatment was unnecessary and that home care was more appropriate; moreover, "a due amount of persuasion" (p. 40) was used to convince the relative to accept the patient at home. The design of the study, thus, had two consequences which differentiated those treated in the hospital from those treated at home. First, the hospital defined itself as a less appropriate context for treating the symptoms and the conditions of some patients and may have served to define different frames of reference as to what symptoms justify hospitalization among relatives of home-care and hospital-care cases. Second, by resisting the hospitalization of patients in the home-care cases, the hospital may have communicated a greater lack of willingness to help the relatives of those in the home-care group than to help relatives of those in the hospital-care group during periods of crisis. It is not unreasonable to expect that, once a person is refused help of a particular sort, he is less likely to request it on a second occasion, and this tendency may explain the greater use of the hospital on subsequent occasions by patients in the hospital-treatment group. In sum, we must evaluate rehabilitation on grounds other than hospitalization.

The investigators provide various data that reflect the psychiatric and social functioning of the patients after 6, 18, and 24 months. These data generally show considerable improvement in all groups by the sixth month, with rather little improvement thereafter. In general, the rates of improvement observed during the first 6 months were no larger for one group than for another, and, thus, one form of treatment does not have clearly superior results in comparison to the results of others. Using the criterion of social functioning, we have little justification for choosing one form of care over another.

Finally, we should inquire into the social costs of retaining patients in the community. We can assess these costs to some extent by using data on various burdensome kinds of behavior. The investigators demonstrated that these difficult behaviors decreased substantially by the sixth month, although they occurred very frequently during the initial study period. At the beginning of the study all three groups showed an equivalent level of family and community disturbance. When the patient was removed to the hospital, the family and the community were relieved of these difficulties; when the patient stayed home, these problems continued, although they decreased through time. In Tables 1 and 2 various data from the study of Pasamanick and his colleagues are reproduced; we

TABLE 1

Percentage of Drug and Placebo Patients Evidencing Each of
22 Behaviors Initially and at 6 Months

Patient Is Burdensome Because	Drug Patients Initially	Drug Patients At 6 Months	Placebo Patients Initially	Placebo Patients At 6 Months
Trouble at night	73	4	64	33
Nursing problem	11	—	18	—
Source of worry	51	6	49	11
Worry about safety of others	25	4	27	32
Uncooperative	48	4	39	29
Strain on others	55	18	36	35
Patient's behavior is upsetting	60	9	48	33
Bodily symptoms cause concern	52	21	61	7
Sexual problem	34	2	27	11
Odd speech and ideas	72	8	73	32
Causes trouble with neighbors	16	2	18	4
Upsets household work and routine	61	15	42	27
Interferes with social activities	29	18	21	19
Forced to stay away from work because of patient	36	3	22	5
Forced to stay away from school because of patient	38	5	19	6
Caused you concern generally	84	34	82	56
Physical strain on significant others	57	19	64	39
Requires excessive amount of attention	55	21	36	18
Children ashamed of patient	11	4	17	11
Children afraid of patient	7	7	16	22
Significant others ashamed of patient	18	2	9	7
Significant others afraid of patient	11	2	18	13

can very roughly depict the social cost of retaining the patient in the community by assuming that the data at the two periods shown in the tables reflect the range of disturbance. Unfortunately, the data from the study do not allow us to assess how rapidly the initial symptoms were alleviated. It is clear, however, that disturbing and troublesome behavior was relieved more quickly than was inadequate role performance, which does

TABLE 2

Percentage of Female Drug and Placebo Patients Wholly or Partly
Unable to Perform Specified Household Activities

Unable to	Drug Patients		Placebo Patients	
	Initially	At 6 Months	Initially	At 6 Months
Attend to housecleaning chores	53	35	42	37
Prepare meals	50	26	41	36
Attend to laundry and cleaning	47	30	32	38
Shop for groceries	55	36	46	38
Do other shopping (clothing, etc.)	44	23	32	38
Budget for household	50	40	44	30
Plan daily activities	62	16	32	22
Solve daily problems	63	23	41	18

(Adapted from *Schizophrenics in the Community, An Experimental Study in the Prevention of Hospitalization*, by Benjamin Pasamanick, Frank R. Scarpitti, and Simon Dinitz, pp. 125 and 434. Copyright © 1967 by Meredith Publishing Company. Reprinted by permission of Appleton-Century-Crofts.)

not show comparable improvement. We must keep in mind, however, that these data apply to schizophrenics, who generally maintain a low level of functioning; they do not portray the situation among less disabled groups.

In summary, the data indicate considerable social cost in keeping the patient in the community during the early periods of psychiatric illness; by 6 months the costs are low enough to make hospitalization the less reasonable alternative. These data support either of two policies: (1) emphasis on home care, with maximal services and community aids provided to help alleviate the strain on the family during the period when the costs are highest; or (2) short hospitalization during periods of greatest strain early in the illness, followed by speedy release. The choice of policy depends on the individual circumstances, the services available to relieve and aid the family in home-care situations, and further data which define more specifically the costs and advantages of pursuing one policy rather than another.

An English 5-year follow-up study of 339 schizophrenic hospital patients who returned to the community (Brown *et al.*, 1966) examined the behavior of patients and the impact of their behavior on relatives and the community. This study suggests that community care for schizophrenic patients involves considerable social cost. The investigators found that in the 6-month period prior to the interview, 14 per cent of first admissions and 27 per cent of previously admitted patients showed such behavior as violence, threats, and destructiveness. Thirty-one per cent of first admissions and 49 per cent of readmissions had delusions and hallucinations. Twenty-eight per cent and 45 per cent, respectively, had other symptoms of schizophrenia such as marked social withdrawal, slowness, posturing, and odd behavior. Finally, 41 per cent of first admissions and 47 per cent of previous admissions had other symptoms such as headaches, phobias, and depression. A significant proportion of relatives of these patients reported that the patient's illness was harmful to their health, affected the children adversely, created financial difficulties, and resulted in restriction of leisure activities and of the ability to have persons outside the family visit their homes. Despite these problems, approximately three-quarters of those who were living with a patient seemed to welcome him at home, and another 15 per cent were acceptant and tolerant.

One of the intentions of the investigators was to evaluate the effect of different hospital policies on patient care and functioning. They, thus, compared three hospitals, one of which was known for its community care policies and found that the functioning of patients was much the same in all three. Patients spent less time in the hospital oriented toward community care, but since they were released from the hospital before complete remission of their symptoms, they were more likely to be unemployed when they were in the community, and they experienced difficulties which led to more frequent readmissions to the hospital. Since readmission usually occurred following a period of disturbed behavior and social crisis, such readmissions and crises were more prevalent in the hospital with a community approach. Moreover, relatives of patients in the community-oriented hospital reported more problems than did relatives of patients in other hospitals.

We must view these data in perspective. Because they pertain to the most disabled category of patients, we cannot generalize the results to other psychiatric categories characterized by less social disturbance. Moreover, the adequacy of a community care program depends on the adequacy of the services available outside the hospital, and in the community studied such services were not fully adequate to the task, although they were probably as good as those found anywhere. This investigation does demonstrate, however, that policy changes must be evaluated in terms of their behavioral consequences and problems and not only in terms of administrative statistics.

In a related study J. Grad and P. Sainsbury (1966) tried to compare and evaluate the effects on families of a community care service and of a hospital-centered service. They were able to evaluate outcomes in two relatively comparable communities which had these different services. The investigators measured the amount of burden incurred by relatives both on referral and 3 to 5 weeks later. Approximately two-thirds of the families with severe burdens showed some relief of the original burden regardless of the nature of the service. Among patients presenting a less severe burden, improvement was somewhat higher in the hospital-centered service (36 per cent versus 24 per cent). In general, the investigators found little relationship between psychiatric symptoms and the extent to which burden was relieved in the two services. They did find, however, that patients with depression caused more hardship if treated in a community service rather than in a hospital service. There were other gains in having a hospital-based service because the closest relative felt less anxiety and suffered less interference with social and leisure activities.

In a 2-year follow-up study of the same patients, Grad (1968) found that the hospital-based service was more effective in reducing anxiety and distress among patients' relatives and created fewer financial difficulties for the family. The families in the community care area were much more likely to have problems of all sorts 2 years later than did those who had patients in the hospital-based service. Moreover, young men treated in the community service were much more likely than those in the hospital-based service to remain unemployed for the entire 2-year period. Differences in social outcome are of large magnitude and raise important questions concerning the philosophy underlying a community-based service. After further investigation, the researchers reported that patients in the community-based service were treated more superficially than were those in the hospital-based service. Grad notes the following problems in community-based services.

> Many social problems, especially those of a more subtle nature, were missed by the psychiatrists. First, their home visits were usually necessarily brief because of pressure of work; second, their interviews in accordance with their training and responsibilities and the families' expectations were patient-focused; third, the high social esteem in which doctors are held meant that family members would often either not presume to detain them by talking about their own troubles or feel relaxed enough in their presence to discuss those family trivia which often reveal social conflicts and stresses. (p. 447)

Other investigations support the observation by Grad and Sainsbury that the burden of mental illness on the family is not exclusive to psychotic conditions but, indeed, may be greater in what are regarded as moderate conditions. J. Hoenig and M. W. Hamilton (1967) in their study of burden on the household found that patients with personality disorders and psychogenic but nonpsychotic conditions caused a considerable amount of objective burden. Similarly M. Rutter (1966), in his study of the effects of mental illness on the health of children in the family, observed that the manner in which symptoms affect family interaction is more important than the nature of the symptoms themselves. While psychotic delusions and hallucinations may not have grave effects on the family if the patient is otherwise considerate and kind, neurotic conditions may lead to destructive and treacherous behavior that disrupts family life and has a profound impact on the psychological state of others in the family.

> Parental mental disorder is most likely to be followed by behavioral disturbance in the children when the parent exhibits long-standing abnormalities of personality. The "seriousness" of the illness in terms of neurosis or psychosis is probably not important, but the involvement of the child in the symptoms of the parental illness does seem to be crucial. For example, delusions *per se* do not matter particularly but if the delusions directly involve the child and affect the parental care, it seems that the child is more likely to develop a psychiatric disorder. If the psychiatrist is to be on the alert for those disorders which are likely to have a harmful effect on other members of the family, he must inquire not only about the symptoms but also about the impact of the symptoms on other people. (p. 107)

Other costs of community care are less obvious and more unexpected. M. Shearer and his colleagues (1968), for example, found a very substantial elevation in birth rates among mentally ill women under community treatment policies. Whatever one's view of the desirability of the mentally ill having children, clearly many of these women are unprepared to provide adequate care for their offspring. Also many mentally ill who return to the community lead isolated and lonely lives, but their problems and needs remain hidden, in part because of their isolation from social contacts of any kind. Some of these patients might prosper much more in a good institutional environment than they do within the community.

The studies by Grad and Sainsbury and other investigators warn us that changing administrative policies and modifying psychiatric procedures to a limited extent are not enough to launch a successful community care program (also see Hoenig and Hamilton, 1967). Grad and Sainsbury believe that the essential ingredient in relieving burden is to assure relatives that help is available and that something can be done; this is a reasonable goal within either kind of service. This sense of control, which Grad and Sainsbury imply, has been recognized in other areas of investigation as an important factor in mediating stress response in difficult circumstances (Lazarus, 1966). The investigators further suggest that for certain types of patients in certain social circumstances home care may leave the family with many more problems than hospital care does. But since psychiatric patients are not a homogeneous group, we must study in far greater detail which patients are most likely to flourish in home care and under what social and psychological circumstances.

Moreover, if the public's responsibility is to be met, it is necessary not only to change administrative procedures but also to guarantee that adequate services are available to help relieve the consequences of such changes and to promote effective functioning of patients outside the hospital.

Environmental Factors Promoting Effective Performance

The realization that mental hospitalization could produce profound disabilities in patients above and beyond those characteristic of the condition itself was a major stimulus to the community care movement. Different investigators have described these disabilities as institutional neuroses, institutionalism, and so on (Zusman, 1966). There are many indices of this syndrome, but generally it can be recognized by apathy, loss of interest and initiative, lack of reaction to the environment or future possibilities, and deterioration in personal habits. Patients who have been in mental hospitals for a long time tend to be apathetic about leaving the hospitals and returning to a normal life and to lose interest in self-maintenance. Moreover, they lack simple skills such as using a telephone or being able to get from one place to another on their own. For a long time observers believed that this apathy and loss of interest were consequences of psychiatric illness rather than the results of long-term residence in an institutional environment characterized by apathy and dullness.

Erving Goffman (1961) provides one of the most provocative analyses of institutional influences on patients. In Goffman's terms, the mental hospital is a total institution, and its key characteristic is "the handling of many human needs by the bureaucratic organization of whole blocks of people." (p. 6) The central feature of total institutions is the bringing together of groups of coparticipants who live in one place—thus breaking down the barriers usually separating different spheres of life—and under one authority, which organizes the different features of life within an overall plan. People are treated not as individuals but in groups and are required to do the same things together. Activities are tightly scheduled, with the sequence officially imposed from above. Finally, the various enforced activities come under a single rational plan designed to fulfill the official aims of the institution.

In depicting the atmosphere of the vastly overcrowded Saint Elizabeth's hospital, Goffman describes the plight of mental patients in vivid terms. From his perspective, hospitalization in a mental institution leads to betrayal of the patient, deprecates his self-image, undermines his sense of autonomy, and abuses his privacy. Moreover, hospital life requires the patient to adapt in a manner detrimental to his future readjustment to community life, and the career of the mental patient is irreparably harmful to his future reputation. Goffman is indeed sensitive to many of the deprivations of hospital life and to some of the abuses of the large mental hospital. But the view he presents is one-sided and very much organized from a middle-class perspective. Many of the deprivations Goffman points to are not experienced, as he describes them, by many mental patients (Linn, 1968).

Many patients find their hospitalization experience a relief. The community situation from which they come is often characterized by extreme difficulty and extraordinary personal distress. Their living conditions are poor, the conflicts in their life are uncontrollable, and their physical and mental states have deteriorated. Such patients are frequently capable of harming themselves or others, or at least of damaging their lives in irreparable ways. Thus many patients in mental hospitals report that hospital restrictions do not bother them, that they appreciate the physical care they are receiving, and that the hospital—despite its restrictions—enhances their freedom rather than restricts it (Linn, 1968).

Although Goffman made us aware of many aspects of total institutions that can be harmful to patients, we must recognize that total institutions can have good or deleterious effects depending on a variety of factors. Total institutions—hospitals, monasteries, schools—are organizations for changing people and their identities. If a client shares the goals and aspirations of the organization, his experiences in it may be worthwhile and desirable. If the client is an involuntary one and rejects the identity the institution assigns him, residence in such an organization may be extremely stressful and lead to profound disabilities in functioning. Just as the young draftee who rejects the idea of armed force and the authority of the military to govern his life may find basic training a stressful experience and one damaging to his self-concept, so does the hospitalized patient who feels he should not be in the hospital and who resents the regimen imposed upon him find hospitalization a stressful experience. But just as there are many cooperative draftees, so are there many cooperative patients, and it is incorrect to assume that the effect of the hospital on them is damaging.

Total institutions vary widely in character. They differ in their size, their staffing patterns, the organization of life within them, the pathways by which their clients arrive, and their expenditures of money, time, and effort. Goffman, in building a general model of total institutions, attributes to them all characteristics which may be products of particular aspects of the hospital he studied, such as its size or staffing pattern. We have evidence that small hospitals with high personnel-patient ratios and large expenditures perform their tasks better than do those with the opposite characteristics (Ullmann, 1967). Mental hospitals often have deleterious effects on patients for a variety of reasons: (1) patients may be involuntarily incarcerated in order to protect the community from them, but once they are in the hospital little of a constructive nature may be done for them; (2) the hospital may not make sufficient efforts to maintain the patient's interpersonal associations and skills when he is removed from the community, although these may deteriorate if the patient remains in the hospital for a significant period of time; (3) hospitalization may lead to the stigmatization of the patient; (4) the hospital may require adaptations for adjustment to the ward, but such adaptations may be inconsistent with the patterns of behavior necessary to make a proper adjustment to the community. In some hospitals, for example, patients are rewarded for remaining unobtrusive and docile, or they are punished if they attempt to exercise too much initiative. But unwillingness to take initiative may handicap the patient when he returns to the community. Not all total institutions respond in this way, and, indeed, very often the ward staff views the participation and the initiative of patients as signs of improving health. Thus, our attention should focus not on whether a hospital fits the model of a total institution but rather on specifying those aspects of such institutions that affect in various ways their performance.

There are many performance variables by which hospitals may be judged. Traditionally, the major concern has been whether they protected the public and those patients in danger of harming themselves. But increasingly investigators are evaluating the hospital in terms of its effects on the patient's work performance, community participation, self-esteem, sense of initiative, responsibility in performing social roles, reduction of symptoms, and understanding of himself and his illness. Studies of large mental hospitals have concentrated on issues such as how hospitals with many patients can be operated by small staffs and few professional personnel. Thus, I. Belknap (1956) devoted considerable attention to the work system of a large hospital and to the manner in which aides in the hospital developed a reward system for the purpose of maintaining a viable patient work force. In contrast, studies of smaller, private hospitals gave greater attention to interaction among patients and staff, communication problems, and administrative conflicts and their effects upon patients (Stanton and Schwartz, 1954; Caudill, 1958; and for a review of this literature, see Perrow, 1965). With new mental health policies, the tendency for public mental hospitals to decrease in size, and the increased provisions for staffing and maintaining mental hospitals, investigators will now have to address themselves to different issues from those considered in the past. It is no longer sufficient to engage in polemics concerning the inhumane conditions of mental hospitals, although where such conditions exist they must be fought. Instead, we must be concerned with how to organize hospitals and wards to achieve the best possible outcomes for patients. I shall have more to say about this matter in Chapter 7.

Many investigators have observed that patients with long histories of residence in traditional mental hospitals have disability syndromes which result from apathy and lack of participation rather than from the patient's illness condition. One term used to describe this disability syndrome is *institutionalism*. It is difficult to study since some psychiatrists do not believe that illness conditions exist, and thus they see all conditions as institutionally or environmentally caused. Even those who have a psychiatric disease theory do not find it easy to separate the effects of the condition from those of the environment since they believe that these interact in an intricate fashion. To evaluate the nature of the institutionalism syndrome, we must look at some of the research on it.

J. Wing, a researcher studying institutional effects on patients, argues that institutionalism is influenced by three factors: (1) the social pressures to which an individual is exposed after admission to an institution; (2) the pattern of susceptibility or resistance to various institutional pressures which the individual possesses when he is first admitted; and (3) the length of time the patient is exposed to these institutional pressures (1962). To test these ideas, Wing measured as well as possible the extent to which hospital schizophrenics were impaired and then attempted to evaluate how length of hospital stay affected institutionalism among patients with comparable degrees of impairment. He found that patient groups with longer lengths of stay showed a progressive increase in the proportion who appeared apathetic about life outside the hospital. Although marked symptom change did not occur over time, hopefulness and willingness to cope with life deteriorated. In such studies, of course, there is always the danger that the patient's sense of apathy affects whether he is released from the hospital, and, thus, the results may be a product of the selection process. But alongside other findings, these results support the idea that hospitals can produce a sense of apathy and hopelessness among patients. Wing and G. Brown (1961), in a study of three British mental hospitals, showed that different hospital environments encourage institutionalism in varying degrees. Thus, the outcome of residence depends not only on the patient's susceptibility to hospital influences and the length of exposure to such pressures but also on the structure of such influences, which may vary widely from one hospital to another.

In a more recent paper, Wing (1967) argues that the syndrome of institutionalism has three components that are very difficult to separate. First, patients who are long-term residents tend to be selected not only on the basis of their illnesses but also on the basis of their social characteristics. They often do not have strong ties with the community, family, or work, and are vulnerable because of their age, poverty, and lack of social interests and ties. Wing points out that these patients often are not concerned with the problems of personal liberty and restrictions and may find the hospital environment far preferable to community residence since this environment meets their needs and makes minimal demands on them. A. Ludwig and F. Farrelly (1966) point to the same phenomena and argue that the problem of getting hard-core schizophrenic patients out of the hospital results in part from the patients' code of chronicity or their desire to remain there. Ludwig and Farrelly's argument is well described by the statement of a schizophrenic patient who told them, "You can't railroad me out of here."

A second aspect of institutionalism, Wing argues, is the inherent unfolding of the disease process itself.

> The bowed head and shoulders, the shuffling gait, the apathetic faces, the social withdrawal and disinterest, the loss of spontaneity, initiative and individuality described so graphically by Barton may be seen in patients who have never been in an institution in their lives. Studies of intellectual performance seem to show that the damage is often relatively sudden in onset, rather than gradual in development as would be the case if it were the result of imposed social isolation. There is little evidence either of gradual clinical deterioration. This is not to say, of course, that the social surroundings do not affect clinical state; indeed, there is evidence to the contrary. (p. 8)

The third component of institutionalism described by Wing is the influence of the institution itself, which gradually affects the patient over many years. This aspect of the syndrome is characterized by increasing dependence on institutional life and an inability to adapt to any other living situation. As Wing points out, these effects can be observed even on patients "whose premorbid personality was lively and sociable and in whom the disease has not run a severe course." (p. 9) Many studies indicate that a large proportion of patients in mental hospitals in the United States and other countries show no serious disturbance of behavior and are kept in the hospital for largely social reasons—many of which are attributable to institutionalism (Ullmann, 1967; Scheff, 1963; Brown, 1959). K. W. Cross and his colleagues (1957), in a survey of a large mental hospital, found that most of the patients had been under care for a long time and that a majority required only routine supervision. The supervisory character of the hospital was as much a product of tradition as it was a response to the needs of patients. A. B. Cooper and D. F. Early (1961) also concluded, on the basis of their survey of more than 1,000 long-term patients, that most did not require custodial care and that a majority could work. In short, many of the traditional practices of mental hospitals have failed to encourage patients to take initiative and responsibility and have sadly contributed to the institutionalism syndrome.

In a study by the author of two facilities for alcoholics in North Carolina, the influence of the environment was found to be extremely important in affecting the patients' attitudes toward rehabilitation (Mechanic, 1961). One of the facilities studied accepted only voluntary patients and was organized around the idea of milieu therapy, making frequent use of group meetings in which patients discussed their problems with one another and with therapeutic personnel. The second facility was a custodial ward for alcoholics and drug addicts in a state mental hospital; most patients were committed to the hospital against their wishes. Patients living within these two different group atmospheres held very different attitudes toward the institution and their own rehabilitation. Thus, although most patients at the voluntary facility verbalized desires for rehabilitation and a commitment to stop drinking, more than a third of the patients at the hospital facility indicated no desire or intention to change their pattern of behavior, and the attitudes of both patients and staff toward rehabilitation could be characterized as cynical. A small group of patients on this hospital ward had entered the hospital on their own initiative to obtain assistance for their alcohol problems; they were very similar in social characteristics to patients at the voluntary facility. We found that more than half of these patients intended to resume drinking after leaving the hospital and were pessimistic about rehabilitation. Although this was not a controlled experiment, the results strongly supported the idea that the atmosphere, group pressures, and attitudes on the ward had an important effect on the attitudes of the patients toward rehabilitation.

Many investigators have been impressed with the importance of the atmosphere of the ward on the functioning and attitudes of mental patients (Stanton and Schwartz, 1954; Kellam *et al.*, 1966), and concern with the influence of environmental atmospheres extends also to other organizations, such as schools and universities. The basic idea is that the emotional tone, tensions, attitudes, and feelings dominant on a ward affect the interactions among patients, between patients and staff, and even among staff. This interaction in turn affects the patient's motivation, attitudes, and emotional state. Thus far, the investigation of these ideas has been largely impressionistic because of the difficulty of measuring different ward environments and correlating these to various performance and symptom measures. Significant progress has been made in the measurement problem by R. H. Moos (Moos, 1968; Moos and Houts, 1968), who has developed scales of psychological environments and is studying a large variety of wards.

Clearly, in acknowledging the detrimental effects of institutions on people, we should not assume that such institutional environments cannot produce rehabilitative effects as well. Mental hospitals, traditionally, have offered patients impoverished environments and have done almost nothing to stimulate them, but this says little about the possibilities of using hospital environments to develop personal skills and resources and to give the patient a new sense of hope (Mechanic, 1967). Mental health workers too frequently make the naïve assumption that community life is constructive, although particular family and community environments may have the same adverse effects on the patient's functioning and skills as a poor mental hospital does. The issue is not so much whether the patient is resident in a hospital as it is whether the environment to which he is exposed is a stimulating and useful one for minimizing incapacities resulting from his illness and for maximizing his potential for living a life of reasonable quality.

A very common observation among persons working with psychiatric patients is that the mentally ill often show impressive remission of symptoms in the hospital but that the symptoms soon reappear when the patient returns to his home context. One view of this phenomenon is that the patient's symptoms reflect particular difficulties he is having at home and when removed from these events he soon improves. However, when he returns to these contexts the problems still remain, and the patient once again demonstrates his failure to deal with them. This situation is particularly acute in the case of children with psychiatric and behavior difficulties, and most psychiatric personnel who work with children feel that it is relatively hopeless to do anything unless one can also have some opportunity to affect the behavior of the child's parents. Psychiatrists have also become interested in working in therapeutic relationships with couples and families on the assumption that many psychiatric problems reflect distortions in roles and conflicts within such units. This assumption, of course, is not shared by all psychiatrists or applicable to all forms of psychiatric illness.

Relatively few studies have examined the community contexts and environments which stimulate the patient's functioning and sense of hope and those which bring a morbid response. In an intriguing study, G. W. Brown, E. M. Monck, G. M. Carstairs, and J. K. Wing followed a group of schizophrenic men released from the hospital (Brown et al., 1962). They assessed the severity of the symptoms of these patients just before discharge, and saw the patients at home with their relatives 2 weeks after discharge. During this home interview they measured the amount of expressed emotion in the family. The researchers found that patients returning to a relative who showed high emotional involvement (based on measurement of expressed emotion, hostility, and dominance) deteriorated more frequently than did patients returning to a relative who showed low emotional involvement. Although it is not entirely clear whether emotional involvement in general or the particular kind measured accounts for the deterioration, this study shows how the family environment is associated with the patient's ability to function. A great deal more work is required to understand the particular interactional and environmental factors which affect the patient's condition and level of disability.

From the point of view of public policy, we should recognize that the construction or modification of effective environments for mental patient care is not exclusively a community or hospital venture. Some patients who have severe psychiatric conditions may achieve a higher quality of life within a sheltered institution than outside one; and in condemning bad institutions we need not abandon the institutional idea entirely since some persons probably function best in them. When the Joint Commission on Mental Illness and Health (1961) recommended that all existing state hospitals of more than 1,000 beds be gradually and progressively converted into centers for long-term care and that no state hospital should be increased beyond that size, they were responding to the assumption that large and impersonal institutional environments cannot provide the individualized attention and environmental atmosphere necessary to overcome institutionalism and to promote the ordinary patient's competence and initiative.

Chapter 7

CONCEPTS AND STRATEGIES OF PREVENTIVE AND COMMUNITY PSYCHIATRY

There has obviously been a tremendous growth in support from governmental and other agencies for the provision of mental health services, manpower training, and research and education. However, the operation of mental health programs has proceeded more on an ideological thrust than on any empirically supported ideas concerning the feasibility and the effectiveness of particular alternatives. Politics being what they are, mental health workers are wise to take what they can get when they can get it. But it would be a tragic mistake if the community mental health movement came to believe its own rhetoric and substituted its propaganda for detailed investigations of the effectiveness of alternative systems of providing mental health care.

Despite the lack of agreement on many issues there is considerable consensus that mental health centers will play an increasingly important role in mental health care; the federal government has already authorized more than 300 million dollars for construction of such facilities. Community health centers originally had three basic roles: (1) treatment of acute mental illness; (2) care for mental patients either prior to admission to a hospital or after discharge from a hospital; and (3) mental health education. With the changing character of mental hospitals—particularly the considerable shortening of hospital stay—the need for a wide variety of continuing community services to help sustain many mental patients in the community is apparent. Yet, several observers are already concerned that community mental health centers are committed less to this goal than to others and, very much like the clinics that previously existed, are devoting their attention to less disabled clients. But the community mental health effort is still very much unformed, and many centers are searching for professional roles and perspectives related to community needs and for an approach consistent with a broad attack on the mental health problem.

Although traditional forms of psychotherapy have dominated mental health practice, their limitations have led mental health professionals to seek new models. In general a growing orientation views the mental health center as the focus of a network of services built around the clinical competence of mental health practitioners but supplemented by a public health approach heavily based on knowledge of the behavioral sciences (Kahn, 1966; Bolman, 1968). More specifically, sophisticated psychiatrists have a strong tendency to view the mental health center not so much as a location as an attempt to integrate the many specialized functions carried out by different community agencies into a coherent pattern. They see such care as being superior to that ordinarily provided and also as being more appropriate to the multiproblem families so typically a focus of one kind of mental health care or another. Seen in this light, the concept of community psychiatry is a very reasonable and modest attempt to apply the principles of public health to mental health and through research and experience to develop technologies which bring defined communities an integrated and high level of service. But other views of community psychiatry do not have modest goals and presume to deliver services well beyond the competence, abilities, and manpower resources of the mental health professions. Although I share the desires of these advocates to improve the quality of services for those who need them, I feel that grandiose and unrealistic claims only breed disappointment and frustration, and handicap the true interests of people in need. Thus, I approach the area of community psychiatry and its accompanying ideology very critically for an area as important as this merits the effort to ferret out valuable ideas and perspectives from much of the prevailing nonsense.

The New Ideology of Community Psychiatry

Conceptions of community psychiatry vary. They range from modest programs to improve community facilities for the mentally ill to extensive programs oriented toward rehabilitating the sick society; from those concerned with preventing the occurrence of mental illness in entire populations to those concerned with rehabilitating already incapacitated patients; and from those that encompass a variety of new roles for the psychiatrist and other mental health workers to those that maintain the traditional concepts of practitioner-patient relationships. At its outer fringe the new ideology of community mental health has lofty ambitions unrelated to what we know or can do. In the words of L. Duhl (1963), a vigorous proponent of the new ideology, "The psychiatrist must truly be a political personage in the best sense of the word. He must play a role in *controlling* the environment which man has created." (p. 73)

Gerald Caplan's (1964) conceptualization of preventive psychiatry has stimulated much of current effort in community psychiatry. In his view, the psychiatrist has three major areas of work: (1) primary prevention, in which he attempts to reduce and control the incidence of mental illness; (2) secondary prevention, which includes the typical activities of psychiatrists in attempting to alleviate psychiatric conditions and to control their duration; and (3) tertiary prevention, in which the psychiatrist attempts to develop community resources and programs that help alleviate the degree of impairment suffered by persons with psychiatric conditions. These notions of preventive psychiatry receive their intellectual stimulus from the field of public health, which has had long experience in altering the environmental conditions causing illness before the exact cause of these illnesses was discovered. Thus we could prevent pellagra because we knew that persons with diets including certain foods did not become ill, even though we did not know the specific vitamin deficiency that caused this illness. Similarly, the famous discovery of John Snow that cholera was transmitted via London's water supply allowed officials to control the spread of this disease well before the cholera organism was discovered. The success of public health measures depends, however, on isolating manipulatable causes of disease and on altering these. For example, we have reason for believing that smoking increases the risks of contracting lung cancer and other diseases, and thus we can attempt to discourage people from smoking in the absence of more specific knowledge on how to remove the harmful substances from tobacco. It is very unclear, however, what causes in the psychiatric area are manipulatable or whether psychiatrists have the knowledge or ability to manipulate those that are. Although we may understand that poverty, slum living, conflict and hostility within families, and other social forces are not conducive to mental health, the failure to deal with these problems has little relationship to psychiatric knowledge or psychiatric roles.

As Caplan sees it, primary prevention involves identifying harmful influences, encouraging environmental forces which support individuals in resisting them, and increasing the resistance of the population to future illness. The program he presents is based on social action and interpersonal action. The social-action program is little more than a form of political psychiatry.

> The mental health specialist offers consultation to legislators and administrators and collaborates with other citizens in influencing governmental agencies to change laws and regulations. Social action includes efforts to modify general attitudes and behavior of community members by communication through the educational system, the mass media, and through interaction between the professional and lay committees. (p. 56)

Caplan cites the area of welfare legislation as one that psychiatrists ought to be involved in.

> In some states, the regulation of these grants [Aid to Dependent Children] in the case of children of unmarried mothers is currently being modified to dissuade the mothers from further illegitimate pregnancies. Mental health specialists are being consulted to help the legislators and welfare authorities improve the moral atmosphere in the homes where children are being brought up and to influence their mothers to marry and provide them with stable fathers. (p. 59)

Clearly, Caplan wishes psychiatrists to become involved in matters, such as morality and values, on which there are many views and differences of opinion. Caplan (1965) also sees psychiatrists extending their focus to problems of personnel selection, placement, and promotion.

> If he accedes to these requests, he will find that he is using his clinical skills and his knowledge of personality and human relations and needs not only to deal with persons suspected of mental disorder, but also to predict the fitness of healthy persons to deal effectively with particular situations without endangering their mental health. He will also be exercising some influence upon the nature of the population in the organization, and hopefully he will be reducing the risk of mental disorder by excluding vulnerable candidates and by preventing the fitting of round pegs into square holes. (p. 6)

Caplan even goes as far as to speculate that a psychiatrist might "exercise surveillance over key people in the community and . . . intervene in those cases where he identifies disturbed relationships in order to offer treatment or recommend dismissal." (p. 79) However, he rejects this role not because of lack of ability or knowledge on the part of psychiatrists but because it would be a distasteful role for most psychiatrists and because of political and social complications. That some psychiatrists do not find this role distasteful is evidenced by the more than 1,000 American psychiatrists who responded to an obviously biased poll by *Fact* magazine which attempted to discredit Barry Goldwater's psychological fitness to run for the presidency of the United States. A lawsuit resulted in a jury decision that Goldwater had been libeled. The willingness of so many psychiatrists to lend their political hand to such an obvious misuse of their expertise significantly discredits the profession and indicates some of the dangers that result when psychiatry becomes too closely associated with political action.

Caplan's concept of social action is unfortunate not only because the idea is naïve but also and more importantly because it draws attention away from and discredits his more valuable concept of interpersonal action—providing environmental and social supports for persons facing a variety of crises. Caplan argues that various crises and transitional periods in the lifespan (such as entering school, having a child, going to the hospital for surgery, moving to a new environment) pose severe stresses which may burden a person's coping capacities and entail a high risk of social breakdown. Caplan believes that during such periods persons have a heightened desire for help and are more responsive to it. Thus, he argues, community psychiatrists should seek out situations in which persons feel vulnerable and provide supportive help and new coping techniques to them. He feels that social breakdowns can be prevented either by intervening in the lives of people and their families during crises or by working through various professionals, such as doctors, nurses, teachers, and administrators, who naturally come into contact with people during such crises. Among the contexts Caplan suggests for such crisis intervention are prenatal clinics, surgical wards, divorce courts, and colleges. He believes that by anticipating crises and providing help it is possible to give people anticipatory guidance and emotional inoculation, which help them cope with threatening events.

There is much of value in Caplan's ideas, but his strong advocacy and lack of qualification undermine their creditability. It is true, as Caplan notes, that the death of a mother may be a harmful influence on a small child and that it is helpful if the father remarries a warm, understanding woman (1964, p. 27). It is not clear, however, how the psychiatrist is to achieve this laudatory goal. Indeed, the greatest weakness of Caplan's entire framework is his failure to specify in any clear fashion the techniques by which mental health professionals are to achieve the many goals he advocates. The entire theory of primary prevention, as described by Caplan, is based on a vague conception that environmental trauma and the lack of coping abilities cause mental illness but, as we have pointed out in some detail, the evidence is not at all secure on these details. Although it is extremely valuable to provide support to those who need it, the assumption that so many common problems require assistance from mental health professionals may indeed encourage excessive dependency and a variety of iatrogenic conditions. As one reads Caplan's books and articles and those of his followers, one is forced to wonder how humans have existed for so long without mental health professionals and without a total breakdown in the social fabric. Indeed, little evidence indicates that the trouble-shooting Caplan advocates has any real impact on the occurrence of mental illness or is directed at those who are likely to become mentally ill if untreated. In short, although we can be sympathetic with Caplan's view that we cannot wait until all the knowledge is in, we must be cautious that we do not invest our mental health resources in fashionable but unproven activities, while those who are really mentally ill go without adequate care or treatment. Finally, we should note that intervention when people have neither sought nor desired our assistance is a serious infringement of the public's privacy. While psychiatrists intervene in persons' lives without their consent when they believe the community requires protection, this intervention is at best a necessary evil. Interference in the lives of normal persons and groups without their consent is a concept that the public should accept only with the greatest caution.

Ironically mental health professionals are developing grandiose plans when there is much basic work left unfinished. Preventive care during pregnancy and adequate postnatal care, which are essential in preventing mental retardation, prematurity, brain damage, and a variety of other difficulties, are still not available to many persons in our impoverished groups. Family planning services and facilities for families with handicapped children are frequently impossible to obtain. It seems prudent to use the technologies that we know are effective and that have relevance to social functioning and psychological comfort rather than to devote our efforts and resources toward solutions that are untested or that have failed in the past to make a difference (see Bolman, 1968). Whatever merit lies behind the enthusiasm generated for community psychiatry, many patients still require hospitalization and other intensive forms of treatment, and many psychotics continue to need extended and repeated periods of institutional care. Any general formulation of mental health policy cannot be relevant or adequate unless it addresses itself not only to less handicapped patients who receive limited outpatient services but also to the many unfortunate people who require continuing care for their disabilities. We must now consider in detail the special problems of this population.

The Development of New Treatment Environments for the Mentally Ill

Traditionally, one of the largest problems in providing mental health care in the community for patients with serious forms of mental illness was the absence of a range of alternatives to use in dealing with the variety of conditions these patients had and their varying levels of disability. For the most part, communities gave the mental health professional two alternatives in such cases: a counseling or psychotherapeutic relationship for the patient within the community or full-time hospitalization. There has been growing recognition of the need for a variety of intermediate solutions that provide greater support and protection than does outpatient therapy but that do not involve such extreme isolation of the patient as is typical of the situation in the mental hospital. This view is particularly buttressed by growing evidence of institutionalism and by the knowledge that mental hospitalization isolates patients from the community to a much greater extent than is necessary and desirable. Also the gulf between the traditional hospital and the community is very large, and many patients who are hospitalized can return to some degree of participation in the community but are not quite prepared for full participation. It has thus been argued that there is a need for helping organizations that are closer to the community than the hospital is but that also provide considerable support to the patient. These ideas are contained in the concepts of transitional communities and partial hospitalization.

The British used transitional communities for the social resettlement in the civilian community of prisoners of war at the end of World War II (Wilson et al., 1952). They found that the readjustment of such men was difficult, and they decided to institute a program to help refit these men for civilian life. They developed Civil Resettlement Units as transitional communities which facilitated the resumption of a civilian role. The purpose was to attempt to neutralize the suspicions of these men toward authority, to allow them to develop role-taking skills appropriate to civilian life but within the supportive environment of the unit, to reestablish their relationships with the home society, and to help them structure their personal goals. Men who went through the program made a better adjustment than did men with comparable experiences who did not.

The halfway house and the community hostel are transitional communities increasingly used in the care of the mentally ill. The halfway house, located within the community, is a relatively small unit housing between 10 and 30 persons. The patients, who share a common situation, provide emotional support for one another; additional supervisory personnel are usually also available. The halfway house is an intermediate solution in that patients who are not prepared to return home or to their jobs or who are too insecure to make their own living arrangements can live in a supportive environment with others who understand their problems, who are tolerant of their difficulties, and who provide emotional support. The hostel, which is frequently used in European countries for housing former mental patients, provides similar support. Both halfway houses and hostels facilitate the relocation in the community of patients who have no relatives or friends willing to assume responsibility for their care. Similarly, these facilities provide therapeutic personnel with an option should they feel that family living arrangements are inappropriate for the patient. These transitional communities also facilitate a later readjustment in which the expatient may try to live completely on his own.

Partial hospitalization refers most frequently to night and day hospitals. The day hospital provides a program for mental patients who live at home or at some other lodging but who spend their days at the hospital. Such institutions relieve the burden on the family and also help keep patients active and involved by providing them with support and other therapeutic services. They allow the patient to retain ties with the community, but they also reduce the psychological and social costs for the community and the patient. When day hospitals began in the United States, they were used as halfway institutions for patients who had been hospitalized. They are now used very largely in lieu of hospitalization (Kramer, 1962). The night hospital, in contrast, is for patients capable of fulfilling work responsibilities but requiring a treatment and supportive program. Through the night hospital the patient maintains productive functioning in the community at the same time that he is able to take advantage of a hospital program.

Intermediate programs are organized in many ways. Some are associated with large state mental hospitals, others with state departments of mental health. Some are run by the Veteran's Administration and public hospitals, others by private mental hospitals or psychiatry departments in general hospitals. Some of these institutions develop independently; others are integrated with a variety of social services for mental patients. Among the more important of such services are sheltered workshops and retraining facilities, aftercare programs, and expatient clubs. The sheltered workshop provides work opportunities and learning experiences under supervision but does not expose the patient to the competitive situation of a normal job. It may allow him to develop his confidence so that he can undertake employment in the community, or it may offer him work opportunities when he might otherwise be unemployed and without any useful activity to involve himself in. Aftercare programs provide support and help for patients who have moved back to the community but who are faced with loneliness, isolation, and other social and psychological difficulties. Expatient clubs meet some of the same needs, giving persons the support of fellow expatients and helping to alleviate the isolation experienced by many who return to the community. Accompanying these changes have been modifications within the hospitals themselves, such as the institution of patient government and the elimination of many of the custodial aspects of the hospital such as locked doors.

In recognizing the development of new treatment situations, we should note that these are not typical of mental health services around the country, and although there are many halfway houses, day and night hospitals, sheltered workshops, and the like, many communities still provide none of these facilities, while large communities may have a few but not the entire array. One of the intents of recent legislation is to coordinate such services through the community mental health center; and as these centers develop, more facilities for intermediate care will be provided. Ideally, every community should have a wide range of services so that mental health professionals can consider the magnitude of the patient's illness and disability in fitting him to the appropriate service.

The Organization of the Developing Mental Health Professions

The explosion of the community mental health movement, stimulated by vast financial support from the federal government, has created many new roles and opportunities in the mental health field. The relationship among professions and the specific responsibilities of each group are very much in flux; each professional group is feeling its way, and the relationships among them are sensitive and changing. Many, such as psychiatry and social work, are undergoing tremendous internal change, while others, like recreational therapy, are searching for an appropriate role. Moreover, each of the groups is not only responsive to the circumstances of its work situation but is also attuned to the definitions of prestige and activity within its own professional structure. Thus, the concept of the harmonious mental health team must be considered and understood in light of the conflict and competition inevitable among these various professional groups.

W. A. Rushing (1964), in a study of the relationships among mental health professionals within a university hospital psychiatric unit, points out that the adherence of professional persons to their own standards may lead to rigid and inflexible responses to the immediate hospital situation. In the context studied he noted that social workers had difficulty adapting to the educational needs of the hospital, while psychologists, who realized that their primary role in the hospital was to administer psychological tests, still tended to identify with academic teaching and research roles. The result was that the daily work situation required responses inconsistent with professional images and led to resentment and conflict. As Rushing so nicely points out, despite the talk about team effort and equality, each of the professional groups strives to achieve prestige, which is a precious commodity within organizations; if some have more, others have less.

> A community of equals is a fiction, particularly a community composed of several different groups. Despite their proclamations to the contrary, it is not likely that psychiatrists will accept their "ancillaries" as their status equals—at least most will not. Consequently, it is probably best to dispense with a myth which "ancillaries" recognize as such. Conflict between myth and reality, especially when the conflict is recognized, may create unnecessary strain. (pp. 258–59)

The situation described above is even more complex in the new mental health centers which have no clear precedents or traditions and whose structure does not so strongly support the medical profession's status as does that of the general hospital. Moreover, as the mental health center assumes various nonmedical roles (such as occupational retraining, behavior therapy based on the principles of learning theory, new crisis intervention techniques developed by social workers) and entertains new perspectives on psychiatric disabilities, the basis of authority will become more unclear; and it is not unlikely that the infighting will become more fierce. Just as these programs pose new potentialities for patients, so they also pose new opportunities and horizons for each of the different mental health professions.

Innovations in Developing Mental Health Manpower

Despite the advances in developing a pool of mental health professionals, the initiation of new programs requires a much larger pool than is available. Thus new programs must consider alternative manpower resources for undertaking the various tasks visualized. In many cases a high level of professional skill is not required, and often a patient has the greatest need for a sympathetic relationship with another person. In many wards in large hospitals a patient often has no single person who takes a close interest in him and whom he can relate to in any significant way. Mental hospitals have made considerable use of volunteers who visit the hospital wards and help create a warm interpersonal atmosphere. Some of these volunteers also undertake therapeutic casework. One significant program in Boston involved the use of college student volunteers who visited the hospital regularly and developed continuing relationships with patients (Umbarger et al., 1962). Such programs not only bring hospital and community closer together but also help interest college students in careers as mental health professionals.

The use of nonprofessional help has its problems as well as its virtues. Hospital staff are not always receptive to outside visitors who may disrupt the ward, interfere with work routines, and even compete with them. Moreover, since volunteers are not within the hospital authority structure, they are not accountable in the same sense that hired staff are. Often such intruders are resented by aides, particularly when they are critical of the organization of the hospital and of the manner in which patients are cared for. If such programs are not to disrupt the functioning of the hospital and the morale of its staff, they must be carefully planned, and volunteers must receive training and supervision to make them aware of the delicacy of the ward situation.

One of the greatest difficulties in providing mental health services is overcoming the apparent cultural and social gap between middle-class professionals and many lower-class patients. Although the gaps and difficulties in communication are sometimes exaggerated, they can pose barriers to the development of adequate programs; mental health professionals must be aware of these problems and be trained to help overcome them. Often, however, the major need of persons having environmental difficulties—and of many of the psychiatrically ill as well—is to have a warm supportive relationship with another person, and it usually does not have to be someone with high professional qualifications and many years of training. Indeed, as some have argued, a helping person with characteristics similar to those of the person receiving help and from the same social environment may provide more meaningful support than would a highly trained mental health professional. Thus various programs supported by the Office of Economic Opportunity and other social agencies are choosing lay persons from the community and training them to provide supportive help to clients. Various program directors who have used such lay therapists feel that this is a worthwhile innovation and an effective way of providing meaningful help within the community. Although we have no hard evidence, individual experiences appear to be favorable, and there is theoretical reason to believe that a person who shares the culture and viewpoints of a client may be in a better position to gain rapport to help him than is a therapist with a very different perspective.

A Further Word on the Use of Psychoactive Drugs

We have already reviewed some of the implications of drug therapy for the management of mental patients and for administrative attitudes toward the retention and release of patients from mental hospitals. Drugs do not cure mental disorders, but they do greatly facilitate the management of many mental patients and make it much easier to treat psychiatric conditions on an outpatient basis. Drugs now play a major role in treating psychoses, particularly schizophrenia and severe depressive conditions, but their usefulness in the treatment of the neuroses and sociopathic and situational disorders is still unclear (Redlich and Freedman, 1966). Considerable evidence indicates that many of the drugs used have effects above and beyond those attributable to placebos and dummy drugs (i.e., those caused by the suggestive impact of the treatment process on the patient), and their usefulness in treating patients cannot be questioned.

Some psychoanalysts reject the use of drugs because they feel that drugs affect only the symptoms and not the underlying condition. These analysts' total commitment to a particular form of treatment, which has considerably less evidence in its support than does drug therapy, makes one wonder if their ardor is not a disservice to the mentally ill. Kräupl Taylor (1966) mildly put it this way.

> Clinical suffering may often be quickly alleviated today, perhaps even to the point of an apparent cure, by modern anti-depressant drugs. Yet the neglect of physical medicine by psychoanalysis has already become an inveterate habit. It is therefore not surprising that we still come across patients who were psychoanalyzed for two years or more, though they are comparable to patients who improved with anti-depressant drugs in two weeks. Neither psychoanalysis nor drugs unfortunately prevent future relapses in these patients. (p. 286)

The closed system of psychoanalysis, its religious fervor, its obliviousness to empirical inquiry, and its stubborn persistence in maintaining a party line have been amply discussed in other contexts and require no further elaboration here (see Taylor, 1966; Frank, 1961). It is encouraging, however, to see the traditional orthodoxy breaking down; increasingly psychiatrists of a psychodynamic persuasion are open and eclectic in their approach and are using drugs in a limited way (Szasz and Nemiroff, 1963).

Since we do not understand the basic processes underlying the major psychiatric conditions, it is not clear how to appropriately categorize the effects of psychoactive drugs. On a very simple descriptive level these drugs are used to energize or stimulate the depressed and inactive patient and to tranquilize the hyperactive and overstimulated patient. But as T. C. Redlich and D. X. Freedman (1966) point out, these conceptions are not fully consistent with what is known about the range of action of various drugs or about their neurobehavioral effects. For example, the tranquilizer is ordinarily thought of as an antianxiety drug because it reduces agitation. But, as Jonathan Cole shows in his well-known collaborative study, such drugs may have effects on a wide range of symptoms varying from withdrawal to hyperactivity. Although we have a great deal to learn about the pharmacological and behavioral effects of drugs, we cannot question that they have a wide range of action and are one of the most useful aids in providing adequate care for the mentally ill. They alleviate psychological distress and help control bizarre behavior, and they also create the conditions in which the other mental health programs we have described can be meaningfully applied.

Some Thoughts on a Theoretical Framework for Viewing the Maintenance of Performance of Chronic Psychiatric Patients

Much of the work with mental patients in the past was based on a view of man as a sponge—as someone who absorbs developmental and environmental stimuli—rather than being based on a perspective which views him as an active agent molding and affecting, to some extent, the conditions to which he is exposed. Thus, much of our psychological vocabulary is phrased in terms of intrapsychic responses to environmental stress rather than in terms of active strivings and social performance. Although all scientific activity must ultimately be based on a deterministic model of some form, social activity is a product of the manipulation and arrangement of symbols. The scope of the symbolic environment in a complex and dynamic society—and even in simple ones—is so vast and so rich that man has considerable opportunity to affect the direction of his life. We can, therefore, gain some advantage by conceptually specifying for psychiatric purposes the active problem-solving aspects of human adaptation, their relationship to the social structure, and their bearing on the rehabilitation of chronic patients.

In considering the meaning of the concept of social and psychological stress, we realize that this term refers to neither stimuli nor reactions in themselves but rather to a discrepancy between a problem or challenge and an individual's capacity to deal with or to adapt to it. This definition makes clear the importance of skill and performance components as well as of psychological defenses, and for this reason I feel it useful to differentiate between the concepts of coping and of defense (Mechanic, 1962b). Coping, as I use the term, is the instrumental behavior and problem-solving capacity of a person to meet demands and goals. It involves the application of his acquired skills, techniques, and knowledge. The extent to which a person experiences discomfort in the first place is often a product of the inadequacy of such skill repertoires. In contrast to coping, defense (as I am using the term) is the manner in which a person manages his emotional and affective states when discomfort is aroused or anticipated. Most psychodynamic and psychological work deals with defense and not with coping. Implicit within the typical psychological approaches is the idea that the links between abilities and performance are obvious or irrelevant and that only the psychodynamics of intra-psychic response remain problematical. This assumption, in my opinion, is an erroneous one; much that is regarded as intrapsychic dynamics can be seen—perhaps more fruitfully—from a skills-abilities perspective. Behavioral scientists are increasingly interested in the role of skill acquisition in processes which traditionally have not been regarded as having skill components. Although there is a substantial literature on skill components in criminal behavior and on the acquisition and use of illegal means (Cloward and Ohlin, 1960), the skill component is now a consideration also in areas ordinarily regarded as psychological (Becker, 1963 and 1967; Wilkins, 1967; Scheff, 1966b). Consistent with this change have been such studies as the one by S. Schachter and J. Singer (1962), which implies the importance of learning how to define internal arousal; and Schachter (1967) has attempted to explain conditions such as compulsive eating as a result of being unable to differentiate hunger from other forms of physiological arousal. In passing, I would like to note that the process of acquiring most of our skills for dealing with threats (most of which are symbolic and interpersonally organized) is usually indirect and informal; and the skills themselves may have no descriptive vocabularies to use in depicting them. Thus these skills may be very unevenly acquired, and we may not easily identify skill deficiencies until extreme situations develop.

From the point of view of an individual faced with a particular crisis, it is necessary to raise at least three central questions: Does he want to deal with the situation? (motivation); Can he deal with it if he wants to? (coping); And can he maintain his emotional equilibrium in the situation? (defense). Each of these dimensions has an equivalent dimension at the community level. For convenience I shall refer to them as (1) incentive systems; (2) preparatory systems; and (3) evaluative systems. By incentive systems I mean community values and the rewards and punishments developed to push activities in particular directions. Preparatory systems attempt to develop skills and competence in persons so that they can deal with social needs, demands, and challenges. These systems include not only schools and other formal learning experiences but also and more importantly the informal learning acquired through family living and peer association. By evaluative systems, I mean the approval and support or disapproval and disparagement resulting from particular courses of activity. I have elaborated each of these concepts elsewhere (Mechanic, 1968), and to expand on them here would take us too far afield. One essential implication, as Caplan (1964) has pointed out, is that intervention techniques devoted to improving responses to situations may occur at the community level as well as at the individual level.

In general, clinicians who work with the psychiatrically disabled emphasize the psychological barriers and techniques and give relatively less attention to the strategies and techniques through which persons deal with tasks and other people. This emphasis is implicit in their psychological bias and in their entire orientation to the patient. Instead of exploring the nature of the patient's difficulties that lead him to seek care or others to insist that he be removed from his social situation, clinicians emphasize early development and relationships. Too often therapy designed to change the patient is undertaken without giving careful consideration to the situation and problems to which he must return, the skills he will require, and the attitudes and feelings about his disabilities among significant others. Although many of an individual's problems in accomplishing difficult tasks or in dealing with the social environment may not realistically be amenable to intervention, mental health workers can help improve patients' coping effectiveness either by changing or modifying their level of instrumental efforts or by helping alter the social conditions under which they live so that their skills are more adequate and their problems less of a handicap.

Irrespective of whether psychiatric conditions are a consequence of neurological, psychological, genetic, or other problems, various social factors can have important effects on the course of a disability. Rehabilitation in contrast to treatment is frequently concerned with manipulating and regulating the context of the illness rather than the illness itself to achieve the best possible outcome given the practical limits of the nature of the condition and the situational contingencies. Rehabilitation is well advanced in physical medicine, where experts have developed ingenious devices which allow persons with serious disabilities to overcome them and to live useful lives. In comparison, the mental health area offers a more difficult and uncertain situation, and experts continue to grope for a feasible model by which rehabilitation may be furthered.

A rehabilitation approach is based on the premise that the person's injury, defeat, or condition is irreversible because of the present state of knowledge and medical technology. The basic concern, then, is to provide devices for the person or techniques for changing his living situation so that his condition, injury or defect results in the least possible disability. Devices which change some aspect of the person and provide him with new skills include artificial hands, seeing-eye dogs, and artificial talking devices for those who have cancer of the larynx and can no longer speak. These new tools help overcome the disability, and a period of training allows patients to adapt to their use. Disability can also be contained by controlling the environment in various ways. Housewives who have disabling conditions can continue to meet role expectations through the installation of kitchen equipment which facilitates housekeeping. Thus, the woman confined to a wheel chair may use kitchen appliances of different height and construction. In short, the operating principle of such rehabilitation attempts is to change the skills and environment of a person so that an irreversible physical condition results in the least possible disability and disruption of patterns of living.

Rehabilitation does not imply that it is desirable to contain disability in contrast to reversing illness conditions. Unfortunately, in many areas we lack the necessary knowledge and the technology to do this, and under such conditions it is important to help people cope within the limits of their condition. Although this point is very obvious, in the area of psychiatric illnesses, where the knowledge to reverse the basic conditions is frequently lacking, rehabilitation efforts devoted to helping the individual live with his condition are sometimes criticized as defeatist. However, until we have a better understanding of the etiology, course, and treatment of most mental illnesses, it may be more reasonable to attempt to contain disability in this area than to pursue cures without any real knowledge of how they are to be achieved.

Since there is little agreement on approaches for community care programs, the decision to provide a program in no sense specifies what is to be undertaken. At one extreme stand those who visualize community care as nothing more than the extension of the various forms of psychotherapy to new categories of people. More commonly, community care is visualized as a form of social work in which a trained practitioner helps the patient and his family weather crises by applying some knowledge of group and psychodynamic functioning or in which the practitioner serves as an ombudsman, helping to bail the patient and his family out of difficulty with official agencies. I suspect that all these approaches supply a certain degree of support and help that mental patients do not ordinarily receive. But they do not necessarily either correspond to the magnitude of the disability these patients often experience or encourage patients to strive more actively to improve their capacities to cope with their environment. I do not want to belittle any support and sustenance offered to these patients since the most elementary forms of such help are so frequently absent from their lives, and we know that even contact with unskilled but sympathetic workers can do much to keep them functioning in the community. But if we are to meet our responsibility to the mentally ill and their families, we must aspire to achieve and accomplish much more than this.

As we consider various alternatives for rehabilitation programs, an educational approach often seems better fitted to the needs of community care than do traditional medical approaches. Successful functioning is due in large part to the way people learn to approach problems and to the practice they obtain through experience and training. Patients frequently lack information, skills, and abilities that are important in satisfactorily adapting to community life. The idea of the neighborhood service center, offering job advice, health and legal assistance, and other informational help, is based on a similar assumption—that many difficulties people experience are a result of deficiencies in skills and lack of the information necessary to seek redress of their problems (Riessman and Hollowitz, 1967). Although improving the patient's capacity to make a satisfactory adjustment to the community is in no way a cure, the acquisition of new and relevant skills can inspire hope and confidence and can increase involvement in other aspects of a treatment program as well. An educational approach focuses more attention and emphasis on the patient's current level of social functioning and less on his past; and it encourages detailed and careful assessment of how the patient behaves in a variety of nonhospital contexts.

Successful social functioning depends on a person's ability to mobilize effort when such effort is necessary, on the manner in which he organizes and applies such efforts, on his psychological and instrumental skills and abilities, and on supports in his social environment. Although social support is well developed within most community care programs, the other facets of social functioning have been relatively neglected.

The mobilization of effort, assuming some level of involvement, may be facilitated by developing personal and social controls which reinforce and encourage good work habits. Traditionally in the care of the mentally ill in America, patients defined as sufficiently sick to require institutional care were defined as too deteriorated to perform in work roles. Instead, they were frequently allowed to sink into apathetic stupor, while their work skills atrophied. Although the attitude toward the work of mental patients has become more reasonable, persons receiving hospital care are often regarded as too sick to pursue meaningful tasks and a very limited scope of such activity is available to the patient in these treatment contexts. The assumption that mental illness is totally incapacitating is reinforced by programs that fail to keep active those aspects of social functioning that can be sustained. Yet, the ability to continue performing meaningful tasks while under treatment can do much to raise the patient's confidence in himself and to encourage persistence in coping efforts.

Organization of effort involves how persons anticipate situations; how they seek information about them; the extent to which they plan, prepare, and rehearse them in a psychological and social sense; how they test problem solutions; how they consider and prepare alternative courses of action should the situation require it; and how they allocate time and effort. When one begins to look at this problem in the case of chronic mental patients, it is astonishing how poorly their efforts are organized. In general psychiatric practice the ineffectual organization of effort often is seen as a byproduct of the patient's condition and not as a basic component of it. Although such ineffectual performance may be an attribute of the illness, improvement in functioning may be valuable for the patient's self-confidence and mental state generally.

One of the difficulties all psychiatric programs face is the inability to obtain a comprehensive view of how the patient behaves in a variety of meaningful social contexts. Since it is usually impractical for mental health workers to follow the patient closely within the community, they must depend either on informants or on information gleaned from ob-servations of the patient's behavior in the clinical context. But the clinical context is a highly artificial one and may produce problems of coping very much unrelated to those that confront the patient in the community (Rapoport, 1960). As clinical contexts are constructed so that they are more characteristic of actual living conditions, accurate assess-ment of the patient and provision of a program fitted to his needs become possible. To return to the work example, it would be valuable if mental health centers could construct work contexts which approximate com-munity work contexts more realistically. This goal has been achieved to some extent in various European countries which provide realistic contexts for evaluation and instruction and where hospitals have been able to contract meaningful work of substantial variety (Furman, 1965).

In one sense a clinic might be viewed as a school in which the edu-cational program, like a good tutorial program, takes into account the social, educational, and psychological needs of the student. From at least one perspective mental patients suffer from inadequate and misguided socialization experiences; they have failed to acquire the psychological and coping skills necessary for reasonable social adjustment. Such failures may be the product of inherited capacities, brain damage, impoverished childhood circumstances, inadequate training for dealing with stress, or a variety of other causes. The source of the difficulty, however, may not be so important as the question of whether it can be remedied with an appropriate program.

One can visualize various advantages in using an educational model in contrast to a medical one. Successful social functioning requires some ability to act as one's own agent, and one of the disadvantages of the medical model is the tremendous dependence the chronic patient develops on physicians, nurses, social workers, and other mental health workers, and on the institution as a physical entity. An educational model is likely to encourage higher expectations concerning personal responsibility and initiative, and its goals are specific in contrast to the diffuseness of general psychiatric approaches. Moreover, the educational model is a familiar one in our society. One of the persistent problems in the expansion of mental health care to new populations is how to reach working-class people. Although all social strata, may not equally share esteem for education, this model is one which persons from all social segments know and have experienced; and increasingly working-class people who aspire to a better life for themselves and their children have defined education as an essential means. Such a model may appeal to working-class patients who feel more comfortable with it than they do with modern psychodynamics. Moreover, patients share in the educational process to a greater extent than they do in traditional medical approaches, and they are more likely to accept the goals toward which they are moving. Although patients also share in psychodynamic therapies, the goals are more diffuse and less relevant to the specific problems patients face than are the goals of the educational approach. The active role of the client toward well-defined and understandable goals within the educational model can stimulate a sense of control over one's life, self-confidence, and competence, and can encourage activity toward self-improvement (Johnson et al., 1967).

There has been considerable experience and research, particularly in England, in the area of industrial rehabilitation (Wing, 1967). In various studies the results of training moderately handicapped, chronic schizophrenics who wanted to leave the hospital were reasonably good. Even older patients who were more resistant to rehabilitation showed some benefit from the program. Hospitals that prepare their patients for industrial rehabilitation show better results than do those which do not. As J. Wing points out, Industrial Rehabilitation Units provide conditions difficult to devise in mental hospitals, such as a realistic industrial setting, a majority of noninstitutionalized workers, and specific training in work habits. Although one should be careful not to exaggerate the results of such training and some of the improvement noted may be the result of the attention these patients receive, the experience with such programs is reasonably promising and is particularly so when they are supplemented with other services.

The author's own experience in sponsoring a research clerical service within a day hospital connected with the Maudsley Hospital, London, supports the experience of others who have developed work programs for chronic mental patients. Although at the time the research clerical unit was set up industrial work, such as soldering units and wiring electric pianos, was available to patients, the hospital was having difficulty finding sufficient clerical work to maintain an office unit. Many of the patients were chronic schizophrenics and severely handicapped, and I suspect there was some doubt that the hospital could run a successful office unit. At the time, I was having considerable difficulty staffing a very large office operation for a national study, and, thus, after pricing the work commercially I made arrangements with Dr. Douglas Bennett and his staff to set up the clerical operation within the hospital. Patients typed and duplicated questionnaires, addressed letters and envelopes, and even signed my name on various correspondence with my permission. An auditing system was devised whereby all work completed by one patient was checked by a second one, and further sample checks were made by me and by the occupational therapist in charge of the work operation within the hospital. The hospital received the commercial rate for the various jobs done, and the patients were compensated for their work at the legally allowed rates. Although I did not systematically study the project itself, it is my distinct impression that the quality of the work was superb and that the rate of error was lower than that which I can reasonably expect from graduate research assistants at universities.*

It was also the impression of myself and others who were in a position to observe the project that the patients received gratification not only from their earnings but also from the work. It provided them with tasks which allowed them to use their skills in a way that they and the staff defined as meaningful. Although the performance was not very good from the point of view of efficiency (i.e., the average time for the production of each unit was much higher than it would be commercially), when the patients were allowed to work at their own pace the quality of performance was high. Thus, hospitals which would like to contract such work would probably have to price the job rather than provide services on an hourly basis. Or they might pay an hourly wage in part subsidized through the rehabilitation program. In any case it seems clear that maintaining such a unit within a mental hospital is a feasible goal and one that provides meaningful tasks to help keep patients active and involved.

No doubt working under sheltered conditions confronts the patient with a somewhat different situation from that presented by working within the community. For many patients, a sheltered situation is a temporary expedient until their psychological state improves and they regain confidence. Other patients, if they work at all, probably require a sheltered situation. The opportunity for the handicapped patient to work in the community depends on various contingencies, such as the state of the employment market and welfare legislation. When manpower is short, employers are more willing to tolerate inefficient workers and those with bizarre mannerisms than they are when manpower is abundant. Similarly, some countries like England have laws which require employers to hire a certain proportion of disabled persons, and such legislation, of course, increases opportunities for the absorption of disabled persons into the work force. Indeed, efficiency is not the most noble of all values, and employers have a responsibility to society and human welfare as well as to the maintenance of profit.

The educational model in contrast to the medical model may also be useful in that it makes the difficulty of patients appear more reasonable to the uninformed, and so it may help minimize the stigma attached to

---

* A letter from Dr. Bennett (December 5, 1968) informs me that the clerical unit has become even more active, doing hospital duplicating and printing, and it is now equipped with I.B.M. punches and a verifier.

the patients' difficulties. Despite a vast educational campaign the concept of mental illness still carries the connotation of insanity, and a large proportion of patients receiving treatment in mental hospitals deny that they suffer from mental illness (Linn, 1968). By emphasizing the normal potentialities of the mental patient, the educational approach may decrease social distance between treatment personnel and patients and between mental health and community contexts. Others probably find mental patients more acceptable when their problems are described in interpersonal terms (as problems of living and of interpersonal relations) in contrast to being described as illnesses of the mind.

In the long run, of course, little is achieved by changing the labels we use without changing our practices. Obviously, the proper organization of an educationally oriented rehabilitation program depends on the attitudes and approaches of mental health workers. To the extent that they nurture the patient's dependency responses, encourage sick-role reactions, and serve the patient rather than motivate him to serve himself, educational efforts are limited. An educational approach must start with the assumption that mental patients either have or can develop the capacities to meet their own needs; through sympathetic attention, encouragement of motivation, and scheduling and reinforcement of mastery experience, we may be able to set the stage for the patient's improvement in social and psychological functioning.

The foregoing considerations of an educational approach in dealing with disabled patients are based on the assumption—by no means proved —that much of the psychological discomfort persons experience results from failure in social functioning. If skills and mastery can be developed so that persons respond appropriately to difficult events in their environment, the experience of successful performance and mastery may in itself help resolve much of the suffering and distress of many mental patients. That such general comments as these do not apply to every patient should require no elaboration. One of the greatest defects of current efforts in mental health rehabilitation is the administrative assumption that the same care can be given to those with a broad and diverse spectrum of social and psychological disabilities. If mental health clinics are to deal seriously with the magnitude of the problems they face, they must develop diversified and flexible services that more realistically approach the needs of their clients.

The Changing Role of Psychiatry

We have already noted how the idea of primary prevention has led some psychiatrists with lofty motives to encourage their colleagues to engage in a program of community action, and I have also commented on some of the difficulties of implementing this call to action. The most central problem is that those who hold this view of community mental health lack sufficient appreciation of the role of value conflict in social life; their views of community processes and how to modify them are greatly oversimplified. Whatever one's opinion of the idea of preventive psychiatry, it is imperative to remember that societies do not ordinarily make psychological comfort and the maintenance of mental health their ultimate goals. Most social systems are prepared to incur serious costs in respect to these values for the sake of other social goals and personal aspirations. Social structures are not simple, and wherever one turns one finds values and goals interpenetrating in a manner which produces conflict and social stress. Health can never be an absolute but is always measured in terms of social aspirations and goals and changing conditions. There is little doubt that we can eliminate a major hazard to health and life by substantially limiting the ownership and use of private automobiles or that we can diminish the rate of pregnancy and mental distress among unmarried girls by dispensing contraceptives more readily and teaching them how to use them properly. We have long recognized that many of the social problems we face are in large part a consequence of the particular values and goals we wish to promote. More often than not we give other social values considerable priority over the value of positive mental health.

In attempting to contribute in new ways, psychiatry has realistic possibilities and alternatives which do not require great transformations of the traditional psychiatric role. Certainly psychiatry as a profession can encourage increasing the availability of resources and personnel for those who seek care, and psychiatrists can develop adequate therapeutic methods helpful to a variety of social, economic, and ethnic groups. Such approaches include transitional communities and the educational model we have already discussed. Similarly, an enlarged perspective that explicitly takes sociocultural forces and organizational influences into account is useful in individual and group treatment. Since the basic goal of psychiatric intervention usually involves helping the patient to understand his difficulties and to cope with them more adequately, the therapist is inevitably involved in reeducation and in providing social support. The implications of a wider perspective for psychiatry are also evident in various suggestions for greater scope in choosing between treatment alternatives, diversified services that better utilize the social resources of the community (and that are more closely geared to the levels of incapacity different patients experience), and a closer relationship, in general, between treatment and community processes.

The nature of psychiatry and its usefulness as an instrument of social facilitation and control provide numerous opportunities to use the profession in areas of social action not directly related to treatment or to the care of patients suffering from psychiatric conditions. Various organizations and community groups would like to use the legitimacy of psychiatry as an aspect of medicine in pursuing their own ends. Through psychiatry it might be possible to detach certain difficult personalities from organizations, to discredit individuals pursuing unpopular causes, to obtain information for the organization which would not ordinarily be accessible, and to justify informal policies and procedures which violate principles of due process. Thus, various organizations have attempted to use expert psychiatric consultation to raise questions concerning the capacities of political and public figures or to spy on the intentions of their members.

S. L. Halleck and M. Miller (1963) point to several uses of psychiatric consultation which raise the important issues of defining the appropriate limits of the psychiatrist's role. They indicate that psychiatrists are increasingly asked to screen out persons with deviant tendencies from organizations, often without the awareness of organizational personnel that psychiatrists are indeed playing this role. They point to various government programs in which psychiatrists were enlisted to provide support and counseling to recruits but at the same time were expected to inform the government which recruits should be dropped from the program. Thus, psychiatrists were put in the role of befriending recruits and developing a relationship of trust with them, but then were using information obtained in this relationship to betray them. Thomas Szasz (1962b), in describing similar practices in the legal area, refers to psychiatric mind-tapping, in which the psychiatrist uses his relationship with a client to obtain evidence later used contrary to the client's interests. Halleck and Miller (1963) provide a particular example of psychiatrists in a large state university being asked to assist administration and police officials in identifying homosexuals.

> A pair of homosexuals were apprehended and then closely interrogated by the police who were interested in learning the names of other deviates on the campus. The police then set out to question each of those named and before long, a list of impressive magnitude had been amassed. The psychiatrist was then asked to examine each of the individuals named as possible homosexuals. (p. 165)

Since psychiatrists inevitably deal with situations which involve social conflict and conflicting social interests, their alliance with one or another party to a social dispute takes on very large importance. Within medicine in general, but particularly within psychiatry, the doctor may serve different needs and different masters, and thus we should clearly understand what role he plays. In a democratic society, in which people's constitutional rights and personal choices are respected, the value and functions of medicine and psychiatry as social institutions have relevance in that they enhance the individual's ability to fulfill his personal and social choices. And physicians have traditionally served as agents of the patient. The ethical principle was that the doctor give first priority to the patient's interests rather than to his own, other parties', or the state's. However, the pressures of organizational life are contributing to the erosion of traditional roles. Inevitably, they will lead to a greater organizational role for psychiatrists. It is not inevitable or necessary, however, that psychiatrists contribute to the misuse of their role or to the erosion of the ethical principles underlying it. When psychiatrists take on organizational tasks, they must insist that they be structured to protect against the use of psychiatry for nonpsychiatric purposes and to enhance the principle of help, which is the most important goal.

Just as psychiatrists may be used by organizations to handle difficult individuals, so may they be used by people to cope with difficult organizations and social institutions. Just as organizations may abuse the proper functions of psychiatry, so may individuals who wish to use the legitimacy of psychiatry to further their own interests. Individuals may thus request psychiatrists to certify psychiatric disability, to support claims for damage done to them, and to provide an excuse or justification for social failure, for violation of law, and for avoidance of specific legal and social responsibilities. Szasz (1962a), who has directed his attention to personal uses of psychiatry as well as to organizational abuses, refers to this tendency to use psychiatry to achieve personal aims not otherwise achievable as bootlegging humanistic values. A common practice in light of legal restrictions on abortion, for example, is to attempt to find psychiatrists who will maintain that the woman's life is endangered if an abortion is not carried out; consequently, a large proportion of all legal abortions are based on psychiatric grounds. Although the psychiatric loophole may be an important one in view of the harshness of the abortion laws, such solutions to the problem do not give persons in the society equal opportunities. The informed, sophisticated, and economically affluent person is much more likely to have access to those who can provide such help than are the less sophisticated and less affluent members of the society. But the less affluent may need such help the most.

Although Szasz is correct in pointing to the discrimination inherent in the above situation, we should not underestimate the importance of maintaining such mechanisms. Our society is a very large and heterogeneous one, and majority groups, in perpetuating their values and enforcing them legally, may create very great hardships for those with different values. The legal system tends to be rigid and fails to take account of the tremendous variances in the emotional makeup and social situations of people. In enforcing standardized codes it sets the conditions for tragic human situations. Since the law is often unbending, these human problems are dealt with through inaction, organizational discretion, and non-enforcement of the legal codes. Organizational discretion provides opportunities for making the legal system more human, but it also tends to violate the principle that all men are equal before the law. The most disturbing aspect of the discretionary process is that it often favors the privileged and the influential more than others and informally sets up varying standards of justice and compassion. Eventually the law itself should take a more compassionate view of men and a greater appreciation of the differences among them. But as long as the law and formal administrative rules are incapable of dealing with the complexity of human situations, informal systems of social organization will inevitably develop, and psychiatry will play an increasingly important part in the derivation of such informal solutions. Precisely for this reason the profession must be fully conscious of its social roles and responsibilities.

Chapter 8

MENTAL ILLNESS, THE COMMUNITY, AND THE LAW

Mental illness creates a variety of problems for the community as well as for the families of the mentally ill. Mentally ill persons may be a nuisance in the community and may disrupt normal social activities; they also may be dangerous or frightening. Moreover, they may be so depressed, disoriented, or deluded that their presence in the community poses serious risks to their own health and welfare. A person with a psychotic depression may be a serious suicide risk, and persons suffering from extreme states of agitation and confusion may undertake actions which seriously harm their own and their families' welfare. Thus, public policies are developed or evolve for removing from the community some mentally ill persons perceived as being in danger or threatening danger and for providing them with treatment or custody.

The community must also determine under what conditions exposing the mentally ill person to ordinary legal procedures violates his rights and violates humanitarian principles as well. It must define when a person is to be regarded as mentally incompetent or when a person accused of a crime should be excused from responsibility because of mental illness. Indeed, under what conditions should a person be regarded as competent to stand trial? Further, under what conditions and by what criteria should a person be deemed competent to make a contact, to make a will, to get married, to have custody of children, or indeed even to drive an automobile? Policies and procedures must establish and specify conditions and standards under which competency to perform these many functions is to be determined (Allen *et al.*, 1968). Also, governmental agencies must specify the conditions under which it is justifiable to keep mentally ill persons from holding sensitive government positions, the circumstances under which it is permissible to deny adoption rights, the conditions under which health and welfare services should be provided to the mentally ill, and many other matters. I cannot deal with all these issues in this chapter, but I will attempt to pose some of the significant questions and dilemmas underlying the response of the social system to problems of mental illness.

The difficulty in establishing clear-cut and coherent policies on these matters should be apparent from what has already been said in this book. Many issues pertaining to the identification, etiology, and care of mental illness remain cloudy, and confusion and lack of agreement apply also to official procedures. Although one may for legal purposes arbitrarily attempt to define mental illness, mental competence, dangerous behavior, and fitness to stand trial, if the behavioral knowledge underlying such concepts is deficient, inevitably the application of these labels tends to be ambiguous and inconsistent. But decisions must be made despite the absence of precise knowledge. Courts and community agencies must muddle through these difficulties and deal with such problems in the best way they can. The fact that we have difficulty defining and predicting dangerous behavior does not mean that members of the community can disregard such patterns of behavior. And the fact that psychiatrists do not agree on the nature and scope of mental illness does not imply that the law can be oblivious to such matters. One of the major issues underlying the approach of the community to the mentally ill is whether such persons can exercise judgment and thus be held responsible for their actions. Social life proceeds on the assumption that a person's activity is rationally motivated and that he should be held responsible in most circumstances for the consequences of his behavior. At the same time we add certain qualifications to such assumptions; in the case of some accidents, for example, we presume the person did harm without intent and was not negligent within the legal meaning of the term. Much debate in the mental health area concerns the point in mental illness at which it becomes appropriate to assume that persons are not responsible for their behavior, are unable to exercise reasonable judgment, or are incapable of making decisions relevant to their own welfare. Translating these problems into concrete policy questions, we must in some fashion resolve the following issues: (1) At what point is it reasonable to involuntarily treat a patient for a psychiatric condition on the assumption that he is unable to appreciate his need for such care? (2) At what point is a person because of mental illness so unable to appreciate the circumstances of his condition that he must be presumed to be legally incompetent or be assessed as unfit to stand trial when charged with a crime? (3) At what point are we to excuse persons from responsibility for unlawful acts on the assumption that their mental state absolves them from responsibility for such acts? I have ordered the questions to take into account their social importance in contrast to their legal import. Much more has been written on the insanity defense than on the other two issues, but in terms of the vast number of persons affected involuntary hospitalization and fitness to stand trial are the two major sociolegal issues affecting the mentally ill.

Responsibility is ordinarily assumed. We do not usually inquire about a person's responsibility for favorable behavior, such as unusual achievements and heroic deeds. When we consider the behavior unfavorably, however, we define the issue as worthy of consideration. Although words like luck and pull imply that a person may not be responsible for his achievements, only in the negative case does such a determination sharply affect the societal reaction to the person in question. From a legal point of view it is usually assumed that all men have the ability to respond as expected to the conventional standards. This assumption of a reasonable man permits the law to some extent to disregard, for purposes of setting standards of conduct, the tremendous variability in capabilities and responses. Abraham Goldstein (1967) states the issue this way.

> A large part of the criminal law, and particularly that part which figures in the insanity defense, holds defendants to a standard of liability which is objective in nature while at the same time speaking subjective sounding words to juries. The objective standard is administered by rejecting evidence that a given defendant was more fearful than most, more moved to anger than most, more suggestible than most. The courts thus make it appear to juries that the fates of reasonable men are being weighed when, in fact, they may be dealing with quite unreasonable ones. (p. 18)

The Problem of Involuntary Hospitalization

Persons suffering from mental illness frequently fail to recognize or to accept the definition of others that they are mentally ill and require treatment. Thus they may be unwilling or reluctant to seek psychiatric assistance and to cooperate in their care. On the assumption that such patients may constitute a threat to others or to themselves, all states provide legally for their involuntary commitment to a psychiatric facility.

Although Virginia enacted a law for the involuntary commitment of mental patients in 1806, for the most part the incarceration of the mentally ill was informally administered until the middle of the nineteenth century. During that period considerable concern arose over the unjustified commitment of sane people to mental institutions, and in 1845 Chief Justice Lemuel Shaw of the Massachusetts Supreme Court laid down the precedent that individuals could be restrained only if dangerous to themselves or others and only if restraint would be conducive to restoration. This principle is the foundation of most state statutes providing for the involuntary commitment of the mentally ill. Although such statutes were instituted to protect the rights of sane individuals, they are sometimes vehicles used to deprive patients who may be suffering from psychiatric conditions of their civil liberties, even when these patients in fact are not a serious threat to themselves or to others in the narrow meaning of these words.

Relatives of patients and others in the community often demand their removal because they feel their behavior is dangerous or extremely disruptive. Such patients often threaten suicide or violence, engage in destructive behavior, or demonstrate grossly bizarre and disturbing symptoms. Some cases leading to hospital admission are cited below (adapted from Brown *et al.,* 1966).

> Mr. A. C. refused to eat the food provided and had various delusions—for example, that people were poisoning him. Before his admission his mother said that he became wild, throwing things about and threatening his parents. (p. 47)

> Mr. A. D. was found wandering by the police. His parents reported that before he left his home he had been breaking up furniture in the house. (p. 47)

> Mrs. A. E. had taken to walking about the house with nothing on, and on the day of admission had walked down the road to see her G.P. with only a night dress on. She felt that she and her house were dirty, and she had been crying and depressed for some days. (p. 47)

> Two weeks before coming to the hospital Mr. A. G. said that he had met God. His mother reported that he had been wild in manner. He read the Bible all night and was excitable and restless. He couldn't sleep and walked into his mother's room at night and wanted to talk to her. He said he wanted to sit on her lap—and why didn't she kiss him like her husband. (p. 47)

> Mr. A. I. had become a social nuisance. He had been walking around at night, and accusing his neighbors of controlling and interfering with his body. (p. 48)

One has to consider only how he would respond to persistent behavior of this kind to appreciate why people in the community demand that mentally ill persons be involuntarily committed to hospitals when they are unwilling to seek help on their own.

A recent study in a New York State community found that a common aspect of commitment cases was the substantial inability of the patient to care for himself in an appropriate fashion (Mariner, unpublished). A large proportion of the patients, as described by doctors, were incapable of adequate social functioning, unable to assess their own need for care, bizarre in affect and behavior, and seemingly out of contact with reality. The investigator felt that these patients if left alone would get themselves into serious difficulty and that they required supervised care.

To bring out some of the problems intrinsic in involuntary hospitalization, I shall consider the procedures in a single state—Wisconsin—which are typical of the situation generally.* Since Wisconsin has been more enlightened than many other states in the area of social welfare and in provision for the mentally ill, the situation there is no worse than elsewhere and probably is somewhat better than average.

The Wisconsin Mental Health Act establishes emergency provisions that permit a police officer to "take into temporary custody any person who is violent or who threatens violence and who appears irresponsible and dangerous." The law also permits the police to take a person into custody on application of three persons if one is a physician who states "that such person has a mental illness, is in need of hospitalization, and is irresponsible and dangerous to himself or others." Such a person may be kept in custody for 5 days or until regular proceedings are instituted. Under ordinary procedures, on application of three adult residents of the state the court appoints two licensed physicians to personally examine the patient and to report to the court the results of their examination. According to statute, the examining physicians must certify whether the person examined is mentally ill (which is defined as a "mental disease to such extent that a person so afflicted requires care and treatment for his own welfare, or the welfare of others, or of the community") and whether he is "a proper subject for custody and treatment."

Under Wisconsin law the court must set a time and a place for hearing the application and see to it that notice is provided to the patient. The names of the applicants requesting the hearing (the "accusers") are withheld. The court if it wishes may withhold notice if it believes it would be without advantage or would be in some fashion injurious to the patient because of his mental condition. The judge has considerable discretion in procedure: He is expected to explain the nature of the proceedings and the "patient's" rights to him, but he is not required to do so if "it is apparent to the judge that the mentality of the patient is such that he would not understand"; the court may, if it considers it in the best

---

* As this is being written, Wisconsin is in the process of revising the state mental health statutes. Many of the suggested revisions are in the direction of those suggested here.

interests of the "patient," appoint a guardian *ad litem* for him; and the judge may release the "patient," may order him detained for observation, or may commit him if he is convinced that the "patient" is mentally ill and a proper subject for custody or treatment. If the "patient" or a relative or friend demands a jury trial, the judge must provide one. He is, however, not required under the law to inform the "patient" of this right.

Although the Wisconsin Mental Health Act can be improved in several ways, if followed conscientiously it offers an "accused" person considerable protection from being "railroaded" into a mental hospital. The difficulty in the administration of such an act, however, is that the pressures on the court and the nature of mental illness make it extremely difficult to adhere to the spirit of the law. As is the case in many other areas of criminal justice, the informal adaptations of the court and the pressures on its operations cause substantial discrepancies between the spirit of the law and its application.

Consider the ordinary conditions under which applications for emergency detention or involuntary commitment are made. Typically, the allegedly mentally ill person is engaging in visible, bizarre behavior, difficult to understand, unpredictable, and in violation of usual expectations and social patterns. Such behavior may cause anguish to his family and frighten those around him. Frequently such a person engages in disruptive behavior, which brings him into contact with the police or personnel from social agencies who initiate proceedings against him. When an application is filed, there is in fact a strong presumption that the person in question requires hospitalization.

Since judges often are extremely busy and they usually assume that such patients are likely to require detention and treatment, many consider it pointless to spend much time on a meticulous examination of each case. Most persons considered for commitment are eccentric and bizarre in appearance and manner. Thus almost invariably some evidence indicates that the "patient" is not an ordinary person. The difference between the "patient" and an ordinary man is often exaggerated by his being an "accused" person, in that others seek to find peculiarities which they can attribute to "mental illness." The judge himself usually has only a limited knowledge of mental illness, and he is unlikely to make subtle distinctions in evaluating the mental state of persons whose cases are presented to him. Even if he is not busy and has time to make a full investigation, he frequently fails to do so since he has faith in the medical model and is likely to depend on the opinions of the physicians appointed to examine the patient. The judge tends to define the physician as an expert in a matter in which he is at best only an amateur, and he is ordinarily reluctant to reject medical advice. Thus, if the medical examiners recommend commitment, the judge may not hold a serious hearing; he may not conceive that he would allow his own observations to countermand the assessment of the medical examiners. With this frame of reference, it is in the interests neither of the alleged patient nor of the court to hold an extensive hearing. The court has other business to attend to, and judges frequently assume that a legal hearing would not be conducive to the patient's mental health (Scheff, 1964a and 1964b). Thus the commitment process has the form of due process of law but is actually vacuous since the decision tends to be predetermined.

If the preceding analysis is correct, then the judgment on committing a patient depends largely on the complaint concerning his behavior and on the recommendations of the medical examiners. Although the law states that one of the examiners should have special training in psychiatry if such a person is available, finding such a person is frequently difficult.* Examiners in some courts have only a limited knowledge of mental illness. Moreover, since the remuneration for such examinations is relatively small, examiners usually do not feel that they are in a position to attempt a detailed examination. Here, too, there is a strong belief that the patient must be mentally ill since he has been defined as bizarre by others, and such examinations frequently are little more than attempts to document peculiarities that can be attributed to mental illness. Since so many of the patients who are involved in commitment proceedings are mentally ill and in need of treatment, it is not surprising that in the superficial inquiry made by medical examiners and judges, others who are dangerous neither to themselves nor to others or who are questionable subjects for involuntary treatment and custody slip into the net. Moreover, since it is generally assumed that treatment in a hospital cannot hurt the patient, the fact that the community finds him difficult to tolerate encourages the examiner to suggest hospitalization. The recommendation is a safe one for the doctor since he does not have to take responsibility for a future disruptive act committed by the patient if he is released to the community. And he is also not exposed to pressures from those who wish to see the patient committed. Similar considerations apply to the judge's decision.

The decision of the court rests on a determination of whether the patient's mental disease is sufficiently serious to require care and treatment for his own welfare, the welfare of others, or the welfare of the community. The assumption is implicit that there are recognizable criteria for determining when an illness requires care and treatment and when such treatment serves the welfare of various parties. In clear-cut cases of

---

* Under the suggested revisions of the Wisconsin statutes, the court, in addition to or in lieu of one of the examiners, "may appoint a clinical psychologist who has a doctorate from an accredited college or university and who has had at least 3 years experience as a clinical psychologist."

disruptive psychoses, the absence of such criteria poses no formidable problems to the court. But in borderline cases no adequate definitions guide the medical examiners or the court. The determination is subject to medical and legal discretion, and where there is discretion there is variability in practice.

The problem is even more complicated from a definitional point of view because the statute provides that only "mental disease to such extent that a person so afflicted requires care and treatment" should lead to commitment. Many medical examiners and judges define mental disease as a condition requiring care and treatment. It is then not clear on what basis involuntary commitment is enforced since many persons suffering from mental disease are harmless and pose no serious threat either to their own welfare or to the welfare of others. One argument for involuntary hospitalization in mental cases, but not in physical cases, is that persons with mental disease cannot exercise reasonable judgment or choice, while patients with other diseases can. However, the mentally ill person's resistance to hospitalization may be far more rational and justified than the diabetic patient's refusal to take insulin or the heart patient's intransigence in conforming to medical regimen. Except in the case of an acute psychotic condition, there is little basis for the all-encompassing argument that the mental patient has no appreciation of what is in his best interest.

Another argument frequently made in this context is that all mentally ill persons—particularly psychotic patients—may be dangerous, and thus involuntary hospitalization is a necessary expedient to protect the community. The absurdity of this argument should be apparent. Any man *may be* dangerous. A person who has become intoxicated is particularly dangerous, especially if he is driving a car. The high accident rate suggests that even sober persons are not incapable of threatening others. Unless it can be demonstrated that mental patients are more dangerous than are other categories of people, the fact that some mentally ill persons are dangerous hardly justifies a blanket policy toward all mentally ill people. All human activity is characterized by a certain element of risk. We do not indefinitely detain persons, except under very special circumstances, simply because we believe that they may at some time in the future in some fashion be a risk to the community.

In practice, however, the courts often do not differentiate being mentally ill from being a fit subject for custody and treatment. And they do not always clearly specify the degree of mental illness required for commitment, thus leaving it to the medical examiners to apply their own criteria. Since persons faced with involuntary commitment have become entangled in social conflict and problems with the community, the examiners have a strong tendency to assume that custody and treatment are necessary. T. Scheff (1964a), in a study of commitment procedures in

Wisconsin, points out that this tendency has been buttressed by various other assumptions of doubtful validity.

1. The condition of mentally ill persons deteriorates rapidly without psychiatric assistance.
2. Effective psychiatric treatments exist for most mental illnesses.
3. Unlike surgery, involuntary psychiatric treatment involves no risks: It either helps or is neutral; it cannot hurt.
4. Subjecting a prospective mental patient to questioning, cross-examination, and other screening procedures exposes him to the unnecessary stigma of trial-like procedures and may do further damage to his mental condition.

On close examination one finds that each of these assumptions is, at most, a half truth. Although many mental patients do require some form of psychiatric care, others require assistance of a kind very different from that ordinarily provided in mental hospitals. Sympathetic support is often more effective in helping a person deal with his problem than is involuntary hospital care, especially since no clearly effective treatment modalities exist in the care of the mentally ill. Moreover, involuntary care in a mental hospital may be harmful to a person's self-esteem and self-concept and destructive to his reputation and social standing. Finally, a person's hospitalization may adversely affect his employment and other social opportunities.

In supporting the violation of due process of law in legal proceedings affecting the mentally ill psychiatrists frequently argue that such procedures expose the patient to unnecessary indignities damaging to his mental condition. But legal procedures, if carried out in a dignified manner, should not necessarily expose the patient to indignities. Thomas Szasz (1961) states the argument well.

> I believe it is possible that such a hearing is traumatic for a person, as it is alleged to be. However, I feel even more strongly that to be placed in an institution without explanations of how one got there, why one got there, and for how long one will be confined, is even more traumatic. The question is not simply whether a given person is "mentally ill" and whether a hearing is "traumatic"—but rather what are our choices as to how we might deal with this person. If in the name of their allegedly traumatic experience we do what we now do—that is, confuse the patient and deprive him of the opportunity to effectively resist the commitment procedure—then I am 100 per cent against it. . . . I think if a hearing is conducted with humanity and with sensitivity, I don't see anything traumatic about it. (p. 288)

Involuntary commitment often takes place in a context of conflicting interests and views and poses under some circumstances serious problems in the violation of civil liberties. We can illustrate some of the issues intrinsic to the problem by reviewing a case that occurred in Wisconsin in

1967 involving a 22-year-old veteran of the armed services living in a manner that can be described as beatnik in the vicinity of the University of Wisconsin in Madison (Simmonds, 1967).

After returning from the armed services, this young man lived for a short time with his parents in northeastern Wisconsin. Contrary to his parents' values, he did not seek employment, stayed out at night, and did not communicate with his wife, who was living in England at the time. These behaviors distressed and worried his parents. In September of the year he moved to Madison and lived with various friends, both male and female. He did not communicate with his parents or his wife. In January his parents came to Madison, presumably to encourage him to change his pattern of living, only to experience an angry and unhappy confrontation.

The parents, distressed by the unconventional behavior of their son, consulted their family physician, who agreed to sign an application to commit him without an examination, even though he had not seen the young man for several years. The parents then consulted the institutional placement coordinator for Dane County; he called the doctor and gave him a choice of immediate arrest or a court order giving notice of a hearing under the state Mental Health Act. The physician chose to have the man arrested as a person "dangerous to himself and others and in need of immediate hospitalization." The coordinator sent the application to the doctor, who provided alleged medical reasons to justify the decision. A judge signed the application at once and relayed the papers to the sheriff for service. One afternoon, without warning, two officers apprehended this youth and locked him up. His friends brought the matter to the attention of the Wisconsin Civil Liberties Union, which challenged the legality of the procedure followed.

It is instructive to consider the evidence provided by the doctor (who did not examine the patient) to justify the decision that the young man was dangerous to himself and others and in need of immediate hospitalization.

> He has seemed very "different" since he returned from the service in July, 1966. He has seemed very touchy, and critical of everything including his parents. On occasions he has very high opinions of himself and unbelievable plans, such as a job with the University of Wisconsin Engineering Department in research with a Dodge Camper provided, then the idea of entering international law. Since July he has had periods of depression and periods of manic exhilaration. (p. 13)

> That the patient is in need of hospitalization and is irresponsible and dangerous to self and others, so as to require immediate temporary detention by reason of his coming to Madison in September of 1966. He has not communicated with his parents or his wife in England. On Janu-

ary 21, 1967, his parents came to Madison, found him living in an apart-
ment strewn with beer cans, shades pulled, with several "Beat-nik" type
people. He used foul and threatening language to his parents. He made
definite threats towards his mother. (p. 13)

Even if we assume the validity of the alleged facts, nothing in the statement establishes that the youth was, in fact, mentally ill, a danger to
himself or others, or in need of immediate temporary detention. The
statement does attest that the youth was leading an unconventional life,
was violating the moral beliefs of his parents, and was unresponsive to
their exhortations to change his pattern of living. But given his age, he
had every right to do so. Consistent with the ruling of the judge, who
granted a writ of habeas corpus, we must conclude that the commitment
procedure used was a violation of constitutional rights and that it deprived the young man of liberty without due process of law. The alleged
expert medical knowledge that provided justification for detention was
based on hearsay and not on an examination of the patient, and the evidence used to justify his detention as a person "dangerous to himself and
others and in need of immediate hospitalization" was inadequate and
deficient. If the petitioners had followed the usual procedures in seeking
commitment and if the youth did not have the assistance of an attorney,
he would probably have been legally committed.

It is essential to state some particular principles. The issue is not
whether the youth in question had psychiatric difficulties. If we take
psychiatric surveys seriously, a large proportion of our total population
has psychiatric difficulties, yet we would not seriously suggest that all such
persons require forced treatment. The issues are whether under the circumstances it was proper for the young man to be subjected to enforced,
involuntary commitment and whether there was a sufficient evaluation of
the facts or adherence to the legal requirements for such a commitment.
Moreover, dubious use of the emergency provisions of the Mental Health
Act, apprehension without notice, and irresponsibility on the part of
the physician raise grave concern over the manner in which commitment laws are sometimes enforced. Many persons affected by this procedure are not so fortunate in having friends who can intervene on their
behalf, and the violation of their rights often does not become visible to
the community.

The process described does not require a villain. The actions of each
of the parties involved, although perhaps ill advised, were probably based
on commendable motives. The parents could not understand their son's
deviance and way of life and, thus, may have been inclined to see this
deviance as a sign of mental aberration. The doctor, acting as an agent of
the family, probably perceived the situation similarly and wished to help
the family in dealing with its problem. Officials, such as the institutional

placement coordinator and the judge, also probably operated with a strong presumption that such deviance is indicative of mental illness and were willing to cooperate with the parents and their doctor. In short, the process actually encourages a shifting of responsibility and a willingness on the part of various actors to cooperate in what is viewed as a reasonable decision by neglecting the niceties of due process.

The case considered also illustrates how conflicts of interests and values can raise the issue of mental illness. Children, for example, often reject their parents' values and patterns of behavior and pursue courses of action and modes of living which threaten and distress the parents. Contrary to showing respect for their parents, they may be sufficiently alienated so that discussions become altercations and lead to the use of foul and abusive language. Parents often threaten their children, and similarly children in protecting their independence may emotionally state their position in a threatening and unpleasant manner. When such conflicts occur, aggrieved parties sometimes characterize the behavior of their adversaries as mental illness. But such conflicts commonly occur in families and in the community, and in themselves they are hardly grounds for the use of involuntary commitment procedures.

Before leaving the issue of commitment, we must consider more closely a point already hinted at but not elaborated—that whatever the statement of legal protections in commitment proceedings, informal procedures often violate their spirit. In a study of commitment procedures in Wisconsin, Scheff (1964b) found that the evidence on which commitment was based was incomplete and that hearings were in fact perfunctory. Medical examiners spent an average of 10 minutes per case in making their examination and almost always recommended detention. It is Scheff's assessment that since the examiner assumes mental illness and devotes insufficient time to the examination to seriously evaluate this assumption, he makes what he regards a safe decision. In timing the length of hearings in various courts, Scheff found large variations. One court devoted an average of 12 minutes to such hearings, while in the busiest urban court having the most such cases, the average length of such hearings was 1.6 minutes.

> In one urban court (the court with the largest number of cases) the only contact with the judge and the patient was in a preliminary hearing. This hearing was held with such lightning rapidity (1.6 minutes average) and followed such a standard and unvarying format that it was obvious that the judge made no attempt to use the hearing results in arriving at a decision. He asked three questions uniformly: "How are you feeling?" "How are you being treated?" and "If the doctors recommend that you stay here a while, would you cooperate?" No matter how the patient responded, the judge immediately signified that the hearing was over, cutting off some of the patients in the middle of a sentence. (p. 22)

Many states do not require that the "patient" be present at the hearing concerning his commitment, and the court may come to a decision concerning involuntary hospitalization in his absence.

It should be emphasized that most patients involuntarily detained in mental hospitals are a serious danger neither to themselves nor to others. In 1962 Scheff obtained a 4 per cent systematic sample of all patients in mental hospitals in Wisconsin and asked the official responsible for each patient's care if it was likely that the patient would harm himself or others if released (Scheff, 1963). Officials rated approximately three-quarters of the patients as unlikely to be a danger. Many of these patients, of course, may have appeared more dangerous when they were first hospitalized. The intensity of their condition may have declined with the passage of time. In the past, when hospital staffing was very inadequate, patients who were not released from the hospital within a reasonable period of time were forgotten despite the subsequent change in their condition. Many of the patients reported on by Scheff were probably long-term inmates, and failure to return them to the community was probably due in large part to the social difficulties involved in their relocation. With new programs in community mental health and new policies on hospital release in effect, such future populations of long-term patients will probably be significantly reduced. At the same time early release of mental patients and the tendency to treat many in the community will probably result in more incidents in which mental patients get into difficulty with the law or other social agencies. All social policies, of course, involve certain gains and certain costs. A prudent social policy attempts to balance these in some reasonable way.

With the change in the direction of mental health services and with increased concern for civil rights and civil liberties in general, traditional modes of commitment have been sharply questioned. The issue that must be resolved concerns the most appropriate social mechanisms for protecting the community and the mentally ill person without depriving the deviant of the rights and liberties due him. The problems I have described of the short-circuiting of due process in commitment proceedings are general problems in the area of criminal justice, and with the prevailing assumptions and limitations of psychiatric manpower available to the courts, such problems are difficult to remedy. Moreover, the commitment process and the ambiguities associated with it provide the community with some flexibility in dealing with difficult situations often not easily resolved in other ways. The involuntary commitment procedure would be abused less, however, if judges were most aware of the varieties of mental illnesses and their development, and were more cognizant of the risks and realities of sending people to mental hospitals. From the perspective of civil liberties commitment procedures should be under greater surveillance by citizen groups concerned with civil liberties as well as the courts, and greater efforts should be made to provide reasonable protection to persons who feel they have legitimate cause to challenge their commitment.

But these responses attack only the symptoms of the commitment process and not its basic difficulty. A more effective approach to the problem would be to ensure that, when patients are placed in custody for their care and treatment, they are offered humane and worthwhile treatment. As the character of psychiatric services improves and community psychiatric care becomes properly organized, it will not be so necessary to force persons to use them involuntarily. Had the youth in the case described earlier been approached sympathetically and with understanding and encouraged to use a good source of help, he might have been cooperative. The process of apprehension and detention in such cases stimulates anger and uncooperative behavior and does much to convince a person in this situation that there is a conspiracy against him. Reasonably approaching a person in difficulty and offering adequate services in his interest would diminish much of the need for legal commitment. Indeed, what has been ironic about commitment procedures is that the person had been removed from the community, presumably for treatment, but has been placed in an institution where very little treatment has been available.

In recent years the proportion of involuntary commitments among all admissions to mental hospitals has substantially decreased, although there continues to be too great a reliance on this mechanism. Even admissions now characterized as voluntary are frequently achieved through pressure and threat. Patients are frequently brought to the hospital by a police officer or are tricked by officials as to their destination. With some time and sympathy the admission could be made much more humanitarian. In Great Britain, where involuntary procedures are used less commonly, it has been found that with sympathy and encouragement it is possible to convince most patients of the desirability of coming to the hospital voluntarily. There are, however, some problem groups such as chronic schizophrenic patients who often fail to appreciate the seriousness of their condition and their need for hospitalization. Even in England, where the majority of patients enter mental hospitals voluntarily, a large proportion of schizophrenic patients require compulsory admission. In one series of schizophrenic patients studied by G. Brown and his colleagues (1966), 43 per cent were admitted on compulsory order. Involuntary commitment is necessary under particular circumstances, but such drastic alternatives should be applied with great caution and tact, and with recognition of the patient's legal and human rights. Among the many reasons for using legal commitment sparingly is the well-known fact that a patient brought to the hospital involuntarily is much less cooperative in treatment than one who comes willingly. Thus, therapeutic interests themselves justify a careful consideration of the use of commitment when no great danger to the community is involved. When we do use compulsion we would do well to adopt the English procedure of requiring periodic reviews of the necessity of continuing hospitalization to ensure that patients deprived of their liberties are not forgotten.

In concluding this section I should note that there is danger of providing too optimistic an outlook. Even if we assume adherence to due process in the use of commitment procedures and even if the quality of treatment undergoes impressive improvement, the community will still demand that certain individuals be removed and treated despite no desire on their part for such care or treatment. Misfits will always frighten or threaten others, and people will always feel that the interests of the community are best served by placing such deviants in custody. Inevitably what is thought to be in the interest of some is not in the interest of others. As long as deviant behavior exists, there will be a need for social mechanisms to contain it, and although progress can be achieved in improving the forms of the mechanisms and making them more humane, the conflicts inherent in the commitment process are but a small reflection of the conflicts inherent in society itself.

Incompetency to Stand Trial

The well-known use of the insanity defense is relatively infrequent in comparison to the decision that a person charged with a crime is incompetent to stand trial. The reasoning behind such a determination is that a defendant must cooperate in preparing his case and must assist in his defense. If he lacks the capacity to understand the proceedings because of a mental disease or mental deficiency, it is unfair to persist with a trial since this would deprive him of rights accorded all defendants.

Although in extreme cases such provisions pose no great difficulty, in many instances the concept of competency is a murky one. The law regards all ordinary men as having similar capacities to appreciate the proceedings against them and to assist in their defense, but actually men vary as greatly in their intelligence and understanding as court proceedings vary in their complexity. Thus the ordinary "normal" man under "normal" conditions may have more or less capacity to assist in his defense. Mental incompetency pertains, however, not to this normal range but to a lack of capacity caused by mental defects or mental illness.

We face here some of the same issues we have faced before. How is one to develop standards for determining when a defendant lacks capacity to understand his situation and to assist his lawyer? Are we to regard such capacity as inherent in the individual regardless of the difficulty of his case or the necessity of his cooperation? Or are we to view it not as an absolute state but as being relative to the defendant's own prior abilities and capacities? Are we to define a somewhat lowered capacity because of mental illness in a defendant of ordinarily high intelligence and deep understanding as incompetence when we define the understanding of a normal man of average intelligence as competence? Persons whose usual performance is impaired may still outperform others who are fulfilling their highest capabilities.

The resolution of the issue depends on how lawyers, judges, and psychiatrists view mental illness and on conceptions of the link between mental illness and competence. Although this matter has not been studied in any detailed way, clearly the response of courts on this issue is highly variable. Theoretically, the defense, the prosecution, or the judge may raise the issue of the defendant's fitness to stand trial. Each may raise the issue for different motives and on the basis of different understandings of the concepts involved. And as with commitment proceedings, much may depend on the determinations offered by psychiatric experts called to testify as to the competence of the defendant. For example, in the case of *Aponte* v. *State,* the following psychiatric views were offered to support the determination of incompetence as stated in the summary of Chief Justice C. J. Weintraub:

> Dr. Brancale testified Aponte's illness has its peaks and valleys. He said, "this man certainly knows his attorney, knows the psychiatrists that have examined him, and remembers the date and knows he is on trial. But underneath all of this I do not think there is a real comprehension of the dilemma." He conceded that Aponte answered questions "at a reasonably intellectual level" and the answers were "responsive," although the witness added, "I think he was beginning to get irrelevant material in there." . . .
>
> Dr. Brunt, on the trial judge's interrogation, said Aponte "intellectually" comprehended his situation, but not "emotionally," that his answers were "intelligently responsive," but "emotionally he is not involved in this in any way whatsoever"; that he could consult with counsel "in a limited way, or in the limited framework of intelligence." In summary, the doctor stated his "guarded" view was that "Intellectually, and as the Judge asked me, he can answer questions intelligently and at the same time his emotional disturbance is such that he would not give or be able to present an adequate defense or help his lawyer because his emotions would not allow him to do so." (Katz *et al.,* 1967, p. 568)

The circumstances in this case were not simple. The defendant was alleged to have murdered a 13-year-old boy for rather bizarre motives, and these circumstances themselves would lead many laymen to view the defendant as mentally ill. Moreover, two psychiatric experts who testified on his behalf believed him to be schizophrenic with homicidal and suicidal tendencies, although they believed he was legally sane. Psychiatric experts testifying for the state found the defendant to be lacking in mental illness from a psychiatric perspective and sane from a legal point of view. Such a contradiction among experts is a frequent occurrence in adversary proceedings. Chief Justice Weintraub on review came to this conclusion.

> Aponte's testimony itself gives no evidence that he could not fairly stand trial. We find therein nothing to suggest that he is unaware of his position. His memory was precise with respect to the homicide and his conduct before and since. His testimony was vivid. He was responsive. (Katz *et al.*, 1967, p. 568)

In this case the defense attorney probably felt that a judgment of incompetence to stand trial would be in the interest of his client. Such judgments can be made for a wide variety of reasons. Sometimes participants feel that this is the most humanitarian route for dealing with the situation. On other occasions the anger of the community is so aroused against the defendant that his attorney wishes to delay the trial as long as possible or until the public interest and emotions have dissipated; or the attorney may just want time to prepare his case more carefully.

We should also note some of the difficulties relating to psychiatric testimony in such cases. In the testimony in support of the defense in the Aponte case, the psychiatric judgment was based not on cognitive understanding or on the actual behavior of the defendant in assisting his attorneys but rather on the defendant's emotional appreciation of his circumstances. Although intuitively we can grasp what the psychiatrist means by emotional appreciation in particularly selected cases, we have no clear criteria for making such judgments, there is great disparity of opinion among psychiatrists on such judgments, and the basis of these judgments is frequently unclear. Thus, conceptually, one may posit discrepancies between a person's cognitive and emotional responses, but from a practical standpoint such judgments are difficult to make, and it is not clear how large a discrepancy is necessary before one can reasonably argue that it is improper for the defendant to stand trial or that it is inappropriate to regard him as responsible.

If a patient is found to be incompetent he is usually sent to a hospital designated for his care and treatment until such time as he is capable to stand trial. J. H. Hess and T. E. Thomas (1963), in a study of such defendants committed to a Michigan state hospital, found that only 105 of 1,010 had been returned to the courts for trial within a 6-year period. They estimated that more than half of these individuals would spend the rest of their lives in the hospital, although in their view most of them could have been returned for trial within a short period of time. They argue that many of these patients were not really incompetent and that when a court or a lawyer intervened they were quickly returned to court for trial.

It would be futile to attempt to make sense of the results of the incompetency process in terms of the substance of the concepts used. Instead, we must recognize that this process, like the commitment process, is used to deal with a variety of situations that confront the community. If a mentally ill person believed to be dangerous commits a minor offense, he may at best be put in custody for a short time under usual legal proceedings and when he has served his sentence be released. But such a person deemed incompetent to stand trial may be kept in a mental hospital for an indefinite period, perhaps for life. A judgment of incompetency to stand trial thus allows for the indefinite detention of persons believed to be dangerous, of those who cannot cake care of themselves, and of those who are public nuisances. The motives underlying this process, however, are not so clear as the preceding remarks suggest. Many such defendants are clearly mentally ill, and lawyers and judges often feel that a determination of incompetence is in their best interest. Critics of the process feel that this legal provision effectively allows the community to deny persons their legal right to a trial, to a determinate sentence, and to due process of law. They point particularly to the fact that a person found incompetent to stand trial might be detained for his entire life and be deprived of his freedom and rights even though he was guilty of no crimes and did not pose a clear-cut danger to the community or to himself (Szasz, 1965a).

The Insanity Defense

When a person is charged with having committed a crime, the assumption that he is a sane and reasonable man prevails unless it can be determined that by reason of insanity or mental defect he is not legally responsible for the wrongful conduct with which he is charged.* The most common criterion, used in approximately 30 states, is the M'Naghten rule, dating back to a case decided in Great Britain in 1843. The rule states

> that every man is to be presumed to be sane, and . . . that to establish a defence on the ground of insanity, it must be clearly proved that, at the time of committing the act, the party accused was labouring under such a defect of reason, from disease of the mind, as not to know the nature and

* Although the law itself is unresponsive to contingencies, the administration of the law is flexible in regard to extenuating circumstances, and considerable discretion is exercised at every level of administration. See Skolnick (1966).

quality of the act he was doing; or if he did know it, that he did not know he was doing what was wrong. (Goldstein, 1967, p. 45)

In addition to M'Naghten, several states and the federal courts use the irresistible-impulse rule, which establishes as a criterion for legal insanity that the defendant have a mental disease which prevents him from effectively controlling his conduct.

The rules used in establishing legal insanity have aroused heated controversy over the years. Many psychiatrists argue that they fail to take account of contemporary psychiatric knowledge and tend to be rigid, unrealistic, and harsh (Glueck, 1963). They maintain that the determination of sanity should depend on whether and to what extent the defendant is suffering from a mental disease or defect. The United States Court of Appeals for the district of Columbia under the leadership of Chief Judge D. L. Bazelon has applied a new rule applauded by many psychiatrists. The Durham rule states that "an accused is not criminally responsible if his unlawful act was the product of mental disease or mental defect." Judge Bazelon hoped that this new rule would permit psychiatrists to testify more fully and easily concerning the defendant's mental condition (Bazelon, 1967).*

A number of criticisms were leveled at the Durham rule. It was contended that it provides no criteria for establishing what mental disease is or under what conditions an unlawful act can be said to be a product of such disease. Thus, although the rule tends to impart authority to the psychiatric expert, it does not provide clearly identifiable criteria for determining what legal insanity is. From the community's point of view, some observers felt that the Durham rule encouraged the insanity plea in a wider spectrum of cases and was undermining the legal assumption of man's responsibility and accountability. In their view, the concept of sickness is taking over the concept of badness. Because responsibility is a philosophical issue and cannot be resolved by scientific fact, such critics felt that a viable social structure must be based on a strong concept of responsibility and that rules like Durham undermine this concept.

Underlying the debate concerning responsibility is a philosophical dispute between those with rehabilitation perspectives and those with punishment perspectives; the latter maintain that it is necessary for the legal system to encourage a strong sense of responsibility by punishing wrongdoing and attempting to deter violations of the law. Those with rehabilitation perspectives think that deviant behavior is more appropriately regarded as sickness than as badness and that treatment is more

* All indications are that the Durham rule has failed to operate effectively in the District of Columbia, in part, because of the lack of cooperation of psychiatrists at Saint Elizabeth's hospital. Faced with a very large patient population and unwilling to take on larger burdens, these psychiatrists, when they testified in court, applied a very restrictive interpretation to the Durham rule (see Arens, 1967).

appropriate than punishment. If persons violate society's codes because of their own tragic human condition, they argue, the proper road to rehabilitation is sympathy and care, not imprisonment. Such persons wish to give psychiatrists a greater role than they have now in the determination of responsibility.

Between the traditional M'Naghten rule and the novel Durham formulation lies the following recommendation of the American Law Institute (Donnelly *et al.*, 1962).

> A person is not responsible for criminal conduct if at the time of such conduct as a result of mental disease or defect he lacks substantial capacity either to appreciate the criminality of his conduct or to conform his conduct to the requirements of law. (p. 750)

The ALI rule clearly establishes that mental disease or defect does not include abnormalities manifested only by repeated criminal or otherwise antisocial conduct. The definition is intended to limit the inclusiveness of the concept of mental illness by excluding persons generally characterized as psychopaths.

Over the years certain assumptions, not always consistent, have been made concerning the meaning of particular words within these rules and the manner in which they are to be construed. Thus, for example, does "knowing the nature and quality of one's act," in the M'Naghten rule, refer only to the ability to cognitively know the law or may it be construed to pertain as well to the ability to emotionally appreciate the meaning of the law? Much of the controversy over these rules is in part based on the breadth of interpretation given to certain words. In a brilliant discussion of the insanity defense, Goldstein (1967) of the Yale Law School maintains that the prevailing assumptions concerning the interpretation of the M'Naghten rule have no adequate support in legal decisions and that the flexibility of the M'Naghten rule is much greater than most lawyers and judges realize. It is not our role here to consider the various legal constructions that can be applied to the language of these various rules, although such matters are important. It is more appropriate to consider the basic issues of public policy underlying them.

As noted earlier, one of the arguments in favor of modification of the traditional insanity defense is that treatment is more meaningful and valuable than punishment as a response to deviant behavior. Implicit in this argument is the notion that a determination of insanity and subsequent treatment in a mental hospital are more humane and productive than imprisonment. But some observers contest this assumption (Szasz, 1963 and 1965a). Given the low quality of care that has been available in mental hospitals and the stigma of mental illness, they maintain that psychiatric hospitalization is not necessarily more humane or useful to society and the individual than is imprisonment. They point to situations in which persons adjudged insane or unfit to stand trial are kept in mental hospitals involuntarily for periods far in excess of the terms they would have served in prison if convicted and given the maximum penalty for the violation in question. Such long periods of detention, they argue, in institutions of low quality offering little more than custodial care, are in reality harsh and inhumane punishments (Goldstein, 1967). Logically, the issues of responsibility and treatment need not be tied together. There is no reason, as Szasz (1963) maintains, why correctional institutions cannot institute sound psychiatric programs directed to providing therapeutic help to inmates. Similarly, the fact that an institution is called a hospital does not guarantee that it provides a therapeutic program or a humane environment.

Further, we have the thorny issues of what is mental illness, when is such illness sufficiently severe to assume that it is unreasonable to hold a person with such a condition responsible for his behavior, and how does one reasonably link the state of a person's personality with a specific wrongful act.

We have already noted the uncertainty of the concept of mental illness. Psychiatrists disagree considerably among themselves on the meaning and applicability of the concept. Such disagreement applies to the assessment of individual patients and also extends to theoretical conceptions of the phenomenon itself. Some psychiatrists regard mental illnesses as particular, identifiable syndromes akin to those found in the ordinary practice of medicine. To others, mental illness is a dynamic concept characterizing the individual's psychological and social adjustment. Some psychiatrists even contend that no concept of mental illness can be judged independently of the norms of conduct set by the community. To some psychiatrists, mental illness is a limited concept applicable only to a small proportion of problems; others use the concept in such a general fashion that they can maintain that almost everyone in some sense is mentally ill. Although such uncertainty may not be an insuperable barrier in the clinical setting, it is hardly tolerable in legal circumstances, where the concept must be used for making dispositions of persons who have offended the rules of society.

Although jurists and psychiatrists may not fully agree on where to draw the line, such matters in any case are appropriately left to judges and juries. The role of the psychiatrist in legal proceedings as an expert witness is to inform the fact-finder who must make the decision—the judge or the jury. In the case of the insanity defense the psychiatrist is asked to offer information relevant to the decision-making process. Too frequently he finds himself providing his testimony in relation to his understanding of the prevailing legal rule rather than attempting to depict in the clearest way possible the psychological state and social circumstances of the defendant. Since the determination of responsibility is properly the function of judges and juries, psychiatrists should provide useful information to them and not attempt to answer the question of responsibility.

The determination of insanity is a social judgment; it is not a scientific issue or one which allows any reasonably scientific assessment. The rationale underlying the use of the psychiatrist as an expert witness is that he has experience with and opportunity to observe the mentally ill and is thus in a good position to inform the jury and judge concerning possible psychological contingencies affecting the defendant's actions. The judgment of whether it is reasonable to regard the defendant as responsible for his behavior cannot be made on technical or scientific grounds. If, for example, a schizophrenic patient is apprehended committing a crime and when arrested is seen to be in a hallucinogenic state, one would be tempted to attribute his unlawful behavior to schizophrenia. However, most hallucinating schizophrenics do not commit crimes, and many nonschizophrenics do. Thus, the fact that schizophrenia is a concomitant of the unlawful act in no sense establishes any causal relationship between them. In some cases, of course, a link is obvious, as when a mental patient hears voices which tell him to commit an irrational and meaningless offense. But in such circumstances one hardly needs a psychiatrist to make the necessary observations.

Basically, the psychiatrist assesses such situations in a manner not too different from that of a layman. He establishes a link between an offense and an illness by observing the irrationality of the act itself, which he then attributes to the illness from which the patient appears to be suffering. He has an advantage over the ordinary layman in that his familiarity with mental illness tends to give him better insight into how a morbid state can become linked with a particular irrational pattern of behavior. But other professionals such as psychologists, social workers, and nurses have similar special experience that may be informative to those who must make the decision. The courts should attempt to obtain the best description possible of all the various circumstances surrounding the case, and perhaps they can best obtain this description if expert witnesses refrain from stating at all whether they believe the defendant to be responsible. Under such circumstances the issue can be properly left to the judge and the jury, who can consider, given the circumstances of the defendant when he committed the act, whether it is appropriate to regard him as responsible for it.

Another alternative, which has been adopted by the English, is to ascertain whether the person is guilty of the unlawful act with which he is charged. If the defendant is found guilty but mentally ill, his condition is taken into account in sentencing. Under the law he may be sent to a hospital rather than to a prison, but he may not be kept there longer than the maximum sentence for the crime for which he has been found guilty. This procedure overcomes the danger that a defendant found guilty of insanity will be held in a hospital for life or for a period exceeding the one he would have served in prison if found to be sane.

As important as the insanity defense may be, the difficulties which have led to so much debate can be resolved by a firm public policy that ensures the rights of the defendant and the meaningfulness of legal labels. If a court finds a person not guilty by reason of insanity or unfit to stand trial and sends him to a hospital for treatment, such treatment should be available in fact as well as in theory. And, because it is generally known that mental hospitals have been little more than custodial institutions, the courts should periodically review such cases to ensure that proper treatment and care are available and that it is appropriate to continue hospitalization. Finally, when the person in question is no longer a clear danger to himself or to others, he should not be detained involuntarily for treatment longer than for the period he would have served had he been found guilty of the crime.

As a final note, we must be careful not to confuse the legal issues of dealing with mentally ill violators with what really goes on in the courts (Blumberg, 1967; Skolnick, 1966; Donnelly *et al*, 1962). As in the general administration of the criminal law, courts do not operate in practice as they do in theory. Talented psychiatrists and lawyers seek to avoid such proceedings, and the courts deal with such cases in a hurried and informal fashion. Careful legal procedures under such conditions are often disregarded, and the patient's civil liberties are often grossly violated.

The Concept of Danger

The community feels a need to remove persons who are believed to be dangerous and who threaten violence. But public conceptions of what kinds of people might be dangerous are not necessarily correlated with the potential danger of such persons. Violence is a fairly common aspect of our society and of our culture and social institutions. However, most individuals who engage in violent, destructive, and other antisocial behavior are in no sense mentally ill unless one defines mental illness by these criteria. In short, every man in society poses some risk to others. But those believed to pose a risk far in excess of what is common and acceptable to the community are described as dangerous. Thus, when a psychiatrist is asked whether a particular patient or defendant is dangerous, he bases his judgment on a probabilistic prediction that a particular person will engage in behavior injurious to others or to the community.

Determinations of what behavior is in fact injurious are also tricky. Many conventional and normal people can injure the community knowingly or unknowingly. A businessman who sells defective products injures the public as does a manufacturer who produces a product inferior from the point of view of safety. For example, until very recently auto manufacturers did not report dangerous defects in their products, although this failure resulted in injuries and deaths. Similarly, many companies have sold defective and inadequately tested drugs and unsanitary foods, while others knowingly pollute our atmosphere and waterways. We do not ordinarily think of such behavior as injurious in a psychiatric sense because it fits in with our social patterns and is easy to understand within the context of our commercial and materialistic values.

When psychiatrists think of dangerous and injurious behavior, they have in mind deviant forms of behavior contrary to the social patterns of the community as they understand them. Thus an adult male who obtains sexual gratification from fondling small children is likely to be thought of as dangerous, while another man who knowingly sells products harmful to public health and safety is thought of as selfish or greedy. Persons likely to attack others with no motive are considered much more dangerous than are those who do so with cause. In any case, very little systematic knowledge allows psychiatrists to realistically predict when a patient is dangerous. They must depend on their clinical judgment and a variety of clinical impressions, most of which have not been studied in any rigorous way.

One very important fact, contrary to the view of most people, is that little evidence supports the stereotype that mental patients are more dangerous than the general population at large (Rappeport, 1967, pp. 72–80). The public's conception is in part a result of the tendency of the news media to give prominence to the former-mental-patient status of persons who commit serious crimes (Scheff, 1966a). This tendency leaves an impression at odds with the statistical reality.

However, some persons are dangerous, and the probability is higher than average that they will commit a violent and irrational act. Whether they are mentally ill or not, we must be able to recognize them so as to provide adequate protection for the community. Perhaps the best predictor of such behavior is a history of having committed such acts, and psychiatrists give this factor great weight in assessing danger. Although their utility is unproven, other criteria frequently used are the repression of normal aggression and the presence of deep feelings of rage, the presence of paranoid delusions or hallucinations, especially when these imply violence, and the admission of the patient that he finds it difficult to control his antisocial urges. Some psychiatrists feel that aggression, particularly that associated with the excessive use of alcohol and drugs, is very dangerous; others give attention to subcultural factors such as the readiness to express aggression (Rappeport, 1967).

Unfortunately little work has been done toward clarifying the meaning of dangerousness. Much empirical work must be undertaken if the community is to justify continuing to deprive persons of their freedom on the basis of an alleged risk of high danger. It will be necessary also to distinguish between symbolic danger and real danger. For example, persons who engage in various deviant patterns of sexual satisfaction, such as the peeper, the person who exposes himself, or the child molester, are presumed dangerous by the community because people do not understand such patterns of behavior and find it difficult to conceive that a normal and rational person can behave in that way. In contrast, people are much less aroused by drunken drivers, in part because it is much easier for them to comprehend how a "normal" person like themselves can find himself in such a situation.

In areas other than the legal one, our society needs assessments of whether persons are reliable or whether there is a considerable risk that they may engage in dangerous behavior. Thus the armed forces must have some assurance that the handling of nuclear weapons and other dangerous tasks are not allocated to unstable persons. Similarly, businesses and industrial firms are concerned that persons in positions of considerable responsibility be able to perform their tasks without endangering others or the company. A schizophrenic pilot is probably too inattentive to fly his airplane safely, and, indeed, such inattentiveness may risk the lives of a great many people. Thus, there are attempts to psychologically and psychiatrically assess the mental stability of potential employees for particular jobs, although the adequacy of these screening programs is in doubt. Concern even extends to the threat that high public officials who are psychiatrically disabled may harm the public because of their illness, but as yet no one has found an adequate way to balance these risks against the political risks of surveillance of mental health and the risks inherent in the imprecise character of psychiatric selection procedures. Much more research and conceptual sophistication are needed in these areas.

Chapter 9

LOOKING TOWARD
THE FUTURE

By any criterion, the past decade can be characterized as one in which vast improvements were initiated in mental health care. One could see a substantial commitment from the federal government to provide more and better care for the unfortunate. The new programs have presented a challenge to the mental health professions to develop new and better techniques in dealing with the problems of patients in lower socioeconomic groups as well as those who are better off and to restructure professional values and practices to be more responsive to community needs. The new government commitment has set into motion a vast propaganda campaign to make the mentally ill more acceptable to the community and to stimulate a sense of responsibility toward persons so afflicted. It has encouraged a developing trend to release persons from mental hospitals at the earliest possible time and to provide additional services within the community; it has supported new contexts for treating mental illness—particularly community mental health centers, but also psychiatric wards in general hospitals, expanded outpatient clinics, and a variety of intermediate facilities such as halfway houses, day hospitals, and sheltered workshops. If the outcome is somewhat chaotic, it is a constructive chaos; and although some of the new concepts will eventually abort, something solid and worthwhile will remain. Rapid social change always produces some confusion, and the view ahead is not always clear.

Now that the ground has been broken for a new pattern of services for the mentally ill, we should assess the gains and errors of the recent past and plan with greater coherence the framework of mental health services that is the best investment for the future. This entire book has attempted to raise the questions and issues that must be considered in planning ahead. In this concluding chapter I shall restate some of the issues discussed earlier and raise new ones which I feel are particularly important in determining future directions.

Despite an extensive educational campaign to urge the public to view mental illness like other kinds of illnesses, not only the general public but also patients themselves are unconvinced. Moreover, they may be right, for mental illness frequently develops and presents itself in a fashion basically different from that characteristic of many nonpsychiatric conditions. The educational campaign is based on what is probably a fallacious idea—that the public's response to the mentally ill is determined by its knowledge and information rather than by its emotional reaction to the conditions under which mental illness becomes apparent. Many psychiatric conditions present themselves to the community in a bizarre, frightening, and disruptive fashion, and people who are exposed to such behavior obviously react differently from the way they do to more common symptoms.

The difficulty with the informational program is evidenced by the reluctance of the mentally ill themselves to accept the point of view perpetuated and by their tendency to consider their difficulties problems with nerves or physical conditions. Psychiatrists with a psychodynamic orientation believe it essential for the patient to recognize the psychological nature of his disorder if meaningful progress is to be made in helping him, but this position may be erroneous and harmful. We now know that many patients can be helped greatly and their symptoms abated by drug therapy and some kinds of supportive care. Their problems do not have to be defined as psychological or psychiatric ones for them to receive or benefit from such help, and trying to urge such a self-definition on them may be doing them a serious disservice. Many patients who have psychiatric difficulties are elderly and not amenable to psychotherapy. To pressure them to redefine their problems as psychiatric ones when they view them within an organic framework not only may serve no practical purpose but also may alienate them from helpful sources of treatment. We must reject the rigid view that a psychiatric patient must see his problem in a psychodynamic perspective. Indeed, the concept of mental illness itself may be dysfunctional, and a more fruitful approach for the patient and his family may be to view his problem as a difficulty in coping with strain or as a difficulty in some facet of his interpersonal relationships or even under some circumstances as a problem with nerves. There is little point and much danger in shaking the patient's perspective, especially if one has no adequate or practical alternative.

The concept of mental illness is probably dysfunctional because it implies to the average person that the entire personality is disordered. To impose such a definition on a person may force him to redefine himself and subject him to redefinition by others. Moreover, it may so undermine his confidence in his abilities that his limited strengths are further retarded. Much of the assistance provided by psychiatric facilities to persons who need help can be made available without communicating that the person is mentally ill or that he must see himself as sick.

The continuing tendency for patients to resist being defined as mentally ill implies that no matter how many facilities are available for treating psychiatric problems, many persons are unwilling to use them. Most people's closest link with the medical world is their usual doctor, and inevitably the general physician is often the first professional to become aware of many psychiatric conditions. Therefore the general physician should know about psychiatric illness and the sources of help available to patients who may need specialized care. General practitioners often do not keep up with developments in psychiatric assessment and treatment, and they are often ignorant of the state and community facilities available for the diagnosis and care of such conditions (Clausen, 1966, p. 50). Moreover, many general practitioners are insufficiently trained to recognize even very serious mental disorders or to recognize the appropriate occasions to use psychoactive drugs or to make referrals. But because general practitioners are key persons in the recognition and care of the mentally ill, attention must be given to increasing their general psychiatric sophistication, their knowledge concerning the use of psychoactive drugs, and their working relationships with community mental health programs. Indeed, new mental health facilities ought to take an aggressive role in making their services available to the general practitioner and in making it clear that they will work with him in an arrangement suitable to his practice. The fact that the general physician in the United States is usually a private practitioner and that new mental health agencies are largely publicly financed complicates this relationship, but with good will on both sides the present situation can be vastly improved.

There are growing doubts concerning the manner in which new mental health centers are developing and the adequacy of some of the goals set for them. Mental health centers should be encouraged to deal with difficult and unattractive cases as well as with those that fit their preferences. If the ideology of community care of mental patients is to flourish, the community mental health center must take its share of the responsibility for providing a coordinated pattern of aftercare services and continuing help to chronic mental patients as well as for dealing with the more common and less serious psychological disturbances and problems in living. Treating the mentally ill successfully in the community involves making many substantive changes in community services as well as in the administrative policies of mental hospitals. If we are going to encourage the early release of mentally ill persons from hospitals and attempt to maintain chronic psychiatric patients in the community, we must be ready to deal with the problems resulting from such policies. Caring for patients in the community involves serious costs as well as advantages; if the benefits of such policies are to be significant, the community mental health center must provide continuing and intensive assistance not only to these mental patients but also to their families.*

Community mental health facilities must not fall into the trap of operating as if all mental disorders are part of the same continuum and amenable to the same forms of care. The term *mental illness* encompasses a vast range of conditions and disabilities which require different approaches and programs. The concept of community care is viable only if mental health agencies take responsibility for devising and making available a wide range of services for patients and their families. Moreover, as community mental health centers come to view themselves as the focus of a coordinated and integrated pattern of care for multiproblem families, the demands for diverse services become even larger, and there is a tremendous need to develop specific and appropriate technologies. Thus, such techniques as behavior therapy or work rehabilitation, which are directed toward removing particular disturbing symptoms or imparting new skills, have a salutary effect and should not be undermined because they fail to produce a vast transformation of the personality of the patient.

Psychiatry has been traditionally concerned with the reality orientation of the patient; it is also appropriate for the community to concern itself with the reality orientations of the psychiatric professions. In planning mental health services we cannot be oblivious to the true limitations of manpower and resources. Facilities must be planned to ensure that essential needs are properly met before areas of larger uncertainty are explored. Although it is useful to maintain a hopeful and enthusiastic outlook, unrealistic claims and proposals unfitted to the resources likely to be available raise false hopes and breed disappointment and disillusionment. Mental health professionals should not promise services and cures they cannot deliver; when such false promises are made there is invariably a day of reckoning.

* As this book goes to press, another book (Susser, 1968) has been published which shares many of the points of view expressed here. It is an excellent volume to be read in conjunction with this book.

In determining the needs of the population for mental health services, we should set priorities in relation to available resources. An all-
inclusive concept of mental illness fails to separate those problems that
necessitate immediate care from those that are mild and transitory, and it
may readily lead to a poor allocation of psychiatric services. The prevalence of the common cold is not the proper measure for estimating the
need for intensive medical services, and broad concepts of neuroses are
not proper criteria for measuring the character of services most essential
in caring for psychiatric illness and disability. We must first put our
resources into those aspects of care that we know are meaningful in reducing morbidity and distress and direct our services to the populations
in greatest need. Given the uncertainties in psychiatry, we should certainly
retain an experimental orientation and model services in a variety of ways,
but in so doing we must be particularly careful that patients with significant disabilities have a meaningful source of care.

There has been far too much acrimony between those favoring a
community approach and those wishing to invest greater resources in
hospital improvement. In recognizing the detrimental consequences of
poor hospitals on patients' levels of functioning, we must refrain from
debasing all hospital care. Many patients suffer from profound disabilities
and may benefit substantially from a well-designed hospital environment
that provides support but encourages a reasonable level of social functioning. In acclaiming the value of community care, we must be aware
that such environments, if not properly developed, can be extremely
damaging to patients and lead to a very low level of social functioning.
There is an obvious need for a rapprochement between those advocating
community facilities and those wishing to improve hospital programs. If
hospitals remain separated from community programs, they are likely to
suffer and to become permanent repositories for patients rejected or neglected by the community services. If the mental health center is to
fulfill its original purpose, it must devote a good bulk of its efforts to
providing services and training for chronic mental hospital patients
attempting to function within the community. Much emphasis is needed
on work training and on the development of other skills; mental health
professionals should encourage private industry to hire persons with mental hospital histories.

The aged, a group we have said very little about in this book, are
a unique problem and require a special approach. With increasing geo-
graphic mobility and changes in the structure of the family, it is difficult
for the family group to retain the aged person within it. Many aged persons find themselves in mental hospitals not because they require such
care but because other facilities are inadequate or unavailable. It does the
mental hospital no good to serve as a repository for aged persons whom

no one wants to care for, and such treatment does not help the aged person to live in a suitable manner. The isolation and other difficulties of the aged are a continuing and growing problem. We should, therefore, assume responsibility for caring for them in a variety of contexts suited to their needs—adequate institutions for the aged, nursing care homes, day hospitals, and hostels.

In applying many new techniques to the care of mental patients, we must be cautious as well as optimistic. Although these techniques can be powerful in relieving the patient's condition and rehabilitating him, they can also have adverse effects. This danger is well recognized in the area of drug therapy; any reliable practitioner attends to the possible dangers and adverse effects from the drugs he prescribes as well as to their benefits. Practitioners, however, who use primarily psychological techniques sometimes see therapy as a one-way street. Although techniques based on psychodynamic analysis and social reinforcement can produce significant changes for the good as claimed, they can also induce adverse effects. Because much of psychotherapy is social influence, it is just as possible to use the influence techniques to achieve changes detrimental to a person's self-image and adaptation as it is to produce self-esteem and adjustment. In the future we must learn a great deal not only about what therapists should be doing but also about what they should not be doing.

We also should not fall prey to the pervasive ideology perpetuated by psychodynamic psychiatry that man is fragile and is very susceptible to breakdown under stress. Although too much stress can be damaging to a person's social development, mastery of the environment often results from practice and experience in dealing with difficult circumstances. To insulate persons from events that encourage the development of new skills and the opportunity to practice them undermines their capacity to deal with adversity and in the long run may be conducive to social and psychological breakdown. A sense of competence and self-esteem is important for successful social and psychological functioning, and we would do well to nurture these qualities.

The future of mental health care is uncertain, but there are some grounds on which to be optimistic. We have the resources to bring improved care to many unfortunate people who suffer from psychiatric conditions. If we have the will we can do much to alleviate suffering and minimize disability. As we learn more about the causes and course of mental illness, the possibilities for prevention and cure become clearer, and our techniques become more elaborate and also more specific. In looking toward the future we must avoid being dogmatic and remain open to new information and new techniques that help fill many of the gaps in our present knowledge. But tolerance can have its excesses as well, and we must encourage the application of rigorous standards to claims and counterclaims. We must learn to pay deference to the facts rather than to those who proclaim them. In the end what we know or do not know about mental illnesses and its treatment will depend less on the grand theorists and more on those modest research workers who do the grubby work day by day, trying to assess what is true and what is false. The psychiatric professions should offer sustenance and help to those who seek it irrespective of the state of the art. But a wise profession learns to separate that which it really knows from the actions it undertakes to meet its socially defined responsibilities and to offer sustenance to the suffering.

Finally, we must never forget that mental health is not the panacea for all our problems and difficulties. Our problems stem not only from psychological insufficiencies but also from poverty, greed, injustice, and social exploitation of the weak by the powerful. Social and economic resources are limited, and society encompasses true conflicts of interests, goals, and values. In striving to improve the level of psychological and social functioning in our society and the quality of services available to the afflicted, we must remember that the many problems we face, of which mental health is only one, must be attacked not only through medical and educational endeavors but also within the context of an improving society, which strives toward greater social justice and a true sense of compassion for the weak and the sick.

SELECTED REFERENCES

ALLEN, R., *et al.*
   1968   *Mental Impairment and Legal Incompetency.* Englewood
          Cliffs, N.J.: Prentice-Hall, Inc.

ANGRIST, S., *et al.*
   1963   "Tolerance of deviant behaviour, posthospital performance
          levels, and rehospitalization," *Proceedings of Third World
          Congress of Psychiatry.* Montreal, 1961, pp. 237–41.

ARENS, R.
   1967   "The Durham Rule in action: judicial psychiatry and psy-
          chiatric justice." *Law and Society Review* 1 (June):41–80.

AUSUBEL, D. P.
   1961   "Personality disorder is disease." *American Psychologist* 16
          (February):69–74.

BART, P. B.
   1968   "Social structure and vocabularies of discomfort: What hap-
          pened to female hysteria?" *Journal of Health and Social Be-
          havior* 9 (September):188–93.

BATESON, G., *et al.*
   1956   "Toward a theory of schizophrenia." *Behavioral Science* 1
          (October):251–64.

BAZELON, D. L.
    1967 "Justice stumbles over science." *Trans-Action* 4 (July-August):8–17.

BECKER, H. S.
    1963 *Outsiders: Studies in the Sociology of Deviance.* New York: The Free Press.

————
    1967 "History, culture and subjective experience: an exploration of the social bases of drug-induced experiences." *Journal of Health and Social Behavior* 8 (September):163–76.

BELKNAP, I.
    1956 *Human Problems of a State Mental Hospital.* New York: McGraw-Hill Book Company.

BLUMBERG, A. S.
    1967 *Criminal Justice.* Chicago: Quadrangle Books, Inc.

BOCKOVEN, J. S.
    1957 "Some relationships between cultural attitudes toward individuality and care of the mentally ill: an historical study," in M. Greenblatt *et al.* (eds.), *The Patient and the Mental Hospital,* pp. 517–26. New York: The Free Press.

BOLMAN, W.
    1968 "Preventive psychiatry for the family: theory, approaches, and programs." *American Journal of Psychiatry* 125 (October):458–72.

————, AND J. WESTMAN
    1967 "Prevention of mental disorder: an overview of current programs." *American Journal of Psychiatry* 123 (March): 1058–68.

BRENNER, M. H.
    1967 "Economic change and mental hospitalization: New York State, 1910–1960." *Social Psychiatry* 2 (November):180–88.

BROWN, G.
    1959 "Social factors influencing length of hospital stay of schizophrenic patients." *British Medical Journal* 2 (December):1300–302.

————, *et al.*
    1962 "Influence of family life on the course of schizophrenic illness." *British Journal of Preventive Social Medicine* 16 (April):55–68.

1966 *Schizophrenia and Social Care*. London: Oxford University Press.

BROWN, G. W., AND J. L. P. BIRLEY
1968 "Social change and the onset of schizophrenia." *Journal of Health and Social Behavior* 3 (September):203–14.

CAPLAN, G.
1964 *Principles of Preventive Psychiatry*. New York: Basic Books, Inc., Publishers.

1965 "Community psychiatry: introduction and overview," in S. E. Goldstone (ed.), *Concepts of Community Psychiatry*, pp. 3–18. Washington, D.C.: Government Printing Office.

CARSTAIRS, G. M.
1959 "The social limits of eccentricity: an English study," in M. Opler (ed.), *Culture and Mental Health*, pp. 373–90. New York: The Macmillan Company.

CAUDILL, W.
1958 *The Psychiatric Hospital as a Small Society*. Cambridge, Mass.: Harvard University Press.

CLAUSEN, J.
1961 "Mental disorders," in R. Merton and R. Nisbet (eds.), *Contemporary Social Problems*, pp. 127–80. New York: Harcourt, Brace & World, Inc.

1966 "Mental disorders," in R. Merton and R. Nisbet (eds.), *Contemporary Social Problems* (rev. ed.), pp. 26–83. New York: Harcourt, Brace & World, Inc.

————, AND M. R. YARROW (eds.)
1955 "The impact of mental illness on the family." *Journal of Social Issues* 11 (No. 4):entire issue.

CLOWARD, R. A., AND L. E. OHLIN
1960 *Delinquency and Opportunity*. New York: The Free Press.

COOPER, A. B., AND D. F. EARLY
1961 "Evolution in the mental hospital: review of a hospital population." *British Medical Journal* I (June):1600–603.

CROSS, K. W., *et al.*
1957 "A survey of chronic patients in a mental hospital." *British Journal of Psychiatry* 103 (January):146–71.

DAVIDSON, H. A.
1967   "The double life of American psychiatry," in H. Freeman and
       J. Farndale (eds.), *New Aspects of the Mental Health Services,*
       pp. 334–44. New York: Pergamon Press, Inc.

DAVIS, J. A.
1965   *Education for Positive Mental Health.* Chicago: Aldine Pub-
       lishing Co.

DEUTSCH, A.
1949   *The Mentally Ill in America.* New York: Columbia Uni-
       versity Press.

DOHRENWEND, B.
1966   "Social status and psychological disorder: an issue of sub-
       stance and an issue of method." *American Sociological Re-
       view* 31 (February):14–34.

————, AND B. DOHRENWEND
in press   "The problem of validity in field studies of psychological dis-
           order," in H. Wechsler *et al.* (eds.), *Readings in Social Psy-
           chological Approaches to Mental Illness.* New York: John
           Wiley & Sons, Inc.

DOLLARD, J., AND N. E. MILLER
1950   *Personality and Psychotherapy: An Analysis in Terms of
       Learning, Thinking and Culture.* New York: McGraw-Hill
       Book Company.

DONNELLY, R. C., *et al.*
1962   *Criminal Law.* New York: The Free Press.

DUHL, L. (ed.)
1963   *The Urban Condition.* New York: Basic Books, Inc., Pub-
       lishers.

ERIKSON, K.
1966   *The Wayward Puritans.* New York: John Wiley & Sons, Inc.

EYSENCK, H. J.
1965   "The effects of psychotherapy." *International Journal of Psy-
       chiatry* 1 (January):99–142.

————, AND S. RACHMAN
1965   *The Causes and Cures of Neurosis: An Introduction to Mod-
       ern Behavior Therapy Based on Learning Theory and the
       Principles of Conditioning.* San Diego, Calif.: R. A. Knapp.

FELIX, R. H.
1967   *Mental Illness: Progress and Prospects.* New York: Columbia
       University Press.

FRANK, J.
1961 *Persuasion and Healing.* Baltimore: The Johns Hopkins Press.

FREEMAN, H., AND O. SIMMONS
1963 *The Mental Patient Comes Home.* New York: John Wiley & Sons, Inc.

FRIED, M.
1964 "Effects of social change on mental health." *American Journal of Orthopsychiatry* 34 (January):3–28.

FROMM, E.
1955 *The Sane Society.* New York: Holt, Rinehart & Winston, Inc.

FURMAN, S.
1965 *Community Mental Health Services in Northern Europe.* Washington, D.C.: Government Printing Office, Public Health Service Publication No. 1407.

GINZBERG, E., *et al.*
1959 *The Ineffective Soldier: Lessons for Management and the Nation.* New York: Columbia University Press. Three volumes.

GLASS, A. J.
1953 "Psychotherapy in the combat zone," in *Symposium on Stress,* pp. 284–94. Washington, D.C.: Army Medical Service Graduate School, Walter Reed Army Medical Hospital.

_____
1957 "Observations upon the epidemiology of mental illness in troops during warfare," in *Symposium on Preventive and Social Psychiatry,* pp. 185–98. Washington, D.C.: Walter Reed Army Medical Center.

GLUECK, S.
1963 *Law and Psychiatry.* London: Tavistock.

GOFFMAN, E.
1961 *Asylums: Essays on the Social Situation of Mental Patients and Other Inmates.* Garden City, N. Y.: Doubleday & Company, Inc.

GOLDHAMER, H., AND A. W. MARSHALL
1953 *Psychosis and Civilization: Two Studies in the Frequency of Mental Disease.* New York: The Free Press.

GOLDSTEIN, A.
1967 *The Insanity Defense.* New Haven, Conn.: Yale University Press.

GRAD, J.
  1968   "A two-year follow-up," in R. H. Williams and L. D. Ozarin
          (eds.), *Community Mental Health: An International Perspec-
          tive,* pp. 429–54. San Francisco: Jossey-Bass.
————, AND P. SAINSBURY
  1966   "Evaluating the community psychiatric service in Chichester:
          results." *Milbank Memorial Fund Quarterly* 44 (January):
          246–77.

GROB, G.
  1966   *The State and the Mentally Ill.* Chapel Hill, N. C.: Univer-
          sity of North Carolina Press.

GROUP FOR THE ADVANCEMENT OF PSYCHIATRY
  1960   *Preventive Psychiatry in the Armed Forces with Some Impli-
          cations for Civilian Use.* Report No. 47, Topeka, Kansas.

HALLECK, S. L., AND M. MILLER
  1963   "The psychiatric consultation: questionable social precedents
          of some current practices." *American Journal of Psychiatry*
          120 (August):164–69.

HESS, J. H., AND T. E. THOMAS
  1963   "Incompetency to stand trial: procedures, results and prob-
          lems." *American Journal of Psychiatry* 119 (February):713–20.

HESTON, L.
  1966   "Psychiatric disorders in foster home reared children of schizo-
          phrenic mothers." *British Journal of Psychiatry* 112 (August):
          819–25.

HOENIG, J., AND M. W. HAMILTON
  1967   "The burden on the household in an extramural psychiatric
          service," in H. Freeman and J. Farndale (eds.), *New Aspects
          of the Mental Health Services,* pp. 612–35. New York: Per-
          gamon Press, Inc.

HOLLINGSHEAD, A., AND R. C. REDLICH
  1958   *Social Class and Mental Illness.* New York: John Wiley &
          Sons, Inc.

HOOVER COMMISSION
  1955   *Task Force Report on Federal Medical Services* (February).

JACKSON, D. (ed.)
  1960   *The Etiology of Schizophrenia.* New York: Basic Books, Inc.,
          Publishers.

JAHODA, M.
  1958   *Current Concepts of Positive Mental Health.* New York: Basic
          Books, Inc., Publishers.

JOHNSON, D. L., *et al.*
1967 "Human relations training as a response to a need for effective and economical psychiatric treatment," in H. Freeman and J. Farndale (eds.), *New Aspects of the Mental Health Services,* pp. 381–91. New York: Pergamon Press, Inc.

JOINT COMMISSION ON MENTAL ILLNESS AND HEALTH
1961 *Action for Mental Health.* New York: Science Editions.

KADUSHIN, C.
1958 "Individual decisions to undertake psychotherapy." *Administrative Science Quarterly* 3 (December):379–411.

———
1962 "Social distance between client and professional." *American Journal of Sociology* 67 (March):517–31.

———
1966 "The friends and supporters of psychotherapy." *American Sociological Review* 31 (December):786–802.

KAHN, A.
1966 "Planning and practice perspectives on the boundaries of community psychiatry," in L. Roberts *et al.* (eds.), *Community Psychiatry,* pp. 165–81. Madison, Wis.: University of Wisconsin Press.

KALLMAN, F.
1956 "The genetic theory of schizophrenia," in C. Kluckhohn and H. A. Murray (eds.), *Personality in Nature, Society and Culture,* pp. 80–99. New York: Alfred A. Knopf, Inc.

KATZ, J., *et al.*
1967 *Psychoanalysis, Psychiatry and Law.* New York: The Free Press.

KELLAM, S. G., *et al.*
1966 "Variation in the atmospheres of psychiatric wards." *Archives of General Psychiatry* 14 (June):561–70.

KOHN, M. L., AND J. A. CLAUSEN
1955 "Social isolation and schizophrenia." *American Sociological Review* 20 (June):265–73.

KRAMER, B. M.
1962 *Day Hospital: A Study of Partial Hospitalization in Psychiatry.* New York: Grune & Stratton, Inc.

LANGER, T. S., *et al.*
1963 *Life Stress and Mental Health: The Midtown Manhattan Study.* New York: The Free Press.

LAZARUS, R. S.
  1966 *Psychological Stress and the Coping Process.* New York: McGraw-Hill Book Company.

LEIGHTON, A.
  1967 "Is social environment a cause of psychiatric disorder?" in R. R. Monroe *et al.* (eds.), *Psychiatric Epidemiology and Mental Health Planning,* Psychiatric Research Report 22 (April):337–45.

LEIGHTON, D., *et al.*
  1963 *The Character of Danger.* New York: Basic Books, Inc., Publishers.

LEMERT, E.
  1951 *Social Pathology.* New York: McGraw-Hill Book Company.

LEMKAU, P.
  1967 "General discussion," in R. R. Monroe *et al.* (eds.), *Psychiatric Epidemiology and Mental Health Planning,* Psychiatric Research Report 22 (April):357–64.

LEWIS, A.
  1953 "Health as a social concept." *British Journal of Sociology* 4 (June):109–24.

LIDZ, T.
  1963 *The Family and Human Adaptation.* New York: International Universities Press, Inc.

LINN, L.
  1967 "Social characteristics and social interaction in the utilization of a psychiatric outpatient clinic." *Journal of Health and Social Behavior* 8 (March):3–14.

——— 1968 "The Mental Hospital in the Patient's Phenomenal World." Ph.D. dissertation, University of Wisconsin.

LUDWIG, A., AND F. FARRELLY
  1966 "The code of chronicity." *Archives of General Psychiatry* 15 (December):562–68.

MACCOBY, E.
  1961 "The choice of variables in the study of socialization." *Sociometry* 24 (December):357–70.

McGHIE, A., AND J. CHAPMAN
  1961 "Disorders of attention and perception in early schizophrenia." *British Journal of Medical Psychology* 34 (June):103–16.

MANIS, J. G., *et al.*
  1964   "Estimating the prevalence of mental illness." *American Sociological Review* 29 (February):84–89.
MARINER, A. S.
  "The physician and the commitment procedure." Unpublished manuscript.
MECHANIC, D.
  1961   "Relevance of group atmosphere and attitudes for the rehabilitation of alcoholics." *Quarterly Journal of Studies on Alcohol* 22 (December):634–45.

———
  1962a "Some factors in identifying and defining mental illness." *Mental Hygiene* 46 (January):66–74.

———
  1962b *Students Under Stress: A Study in the Psychology of Adaptation.* New York: The Free Press.

———
  1967   "Therapeutic intervention: issues in the care of the mentally ill." *American Journal of Orthopsychiatry* 37 (July):703–18.

———
  1968   *Medical Sociology: A Selective View.* New York: The Free Press.
MISHLER, E. G., AND N. E. WAXLER
  1965   "Family interaction processes and schizophrenia: a review of current theories." *Merrill-Palmer Quarterly* 2 (October): 269–316.
MOOS, R. H.
  1968   "Differential effects of ward settings on psychiatric patients." *Journal of Nervous and Mental Diseases* 147 (October):386–93.
———, AND P. S. HOUTS
  1968   "Assessment of the social atmospheres of psychiatric wards." *Journal of Abnormal Psychology* 73 (December):595–604.
MURPHY, H.
  1961   "Social change and mental health," in *Causes of Mental Disorders: A Review of Epidemiological Knowledge,* pp. 280–329. New York: Milbank Memorial Fund.
MYERS, J. B., AND L. BEAN
  1968   *A Decade Later: A Follow-Up of Social Class and Mental Illness.* New York: John Wiley & Sons, Inc.

Noyes, A. P., and L. C. Kolb
1963 *Modern Clinical Psychiatry* (6th ed.). Philadelphia: W. B. Saunders Company.

Ødegaard, Ø.
1965 "Discussion of 'sociocultural factors in the epidemiology of schizophrenia.'" *International Journal of Psychiatry* 1 (April):296–305.

Pasamanick, B., *et al.*
1967 *Schizophrenia in the Community.* New York: Appleton-Century-Crofts.

Perrow, C.
1965 "Hospitals: technology, structure and goals," in J. March (ed.), *Handbook of Organizations,* pp. 910–71. Chicago: Rand McNally & Co.

Plunkett, R. J., and J. E. Gordon
1960 *Epidemiology and Mental Illness.* New York: Basic Books, Inc., Publishers.

Rapoport, R. N.
1960 *Community as Doctor: New Perspectives on a Therapeutic Community.* Springfield, Ill.: Charles C Thomas.

Rappeport, J. R. (ed.)
1967 *The Clinical Evaluation of the Dangerousness of the Mentally Ill.* Springfield, Ill.: Charles C Thomas, Publisher.

Redlich, F. C., and D. X. Freedman
1966 *The Theory and Practice of Psychiatry.* New York: Basic Books, Inc., Publishers.

Reid, D. D.
1961 "Precipitating proximal factors in the occurrence of mental disorders: epidemiological evidence," in *Causes of Mental Disorders: A Review of Epidemiological Knowledge,* pp. 197–216. New York: Milbank Memorial Fund.

Riessman, F., and E. Hollowitz
1967 "The neighborhood service center: an innovation in preventive psychiatry." *American Journal of Psychiatry* 123 (May): 1408–12.

Roberts, N.
1967 *Mental Health and Mental Illness.* New York: Humanities Press.

Robins, L.
1966 *Deviant Children Grown Up: A Sociological and Psychiatric*

Study of Sociopathic Personality. Baltimore: Williams & Wilkins Company.

ROSENSTOCK, I. M.
1960 "What research in motivation suggests for public health." *American Journal of Public Health* 50 (February):295–302.

RUSHING, W. A.
1964 *The Psychiatric Professions: Power, Conflict, and Adaptation in a Psychiatric Hospital Staff.* Chapel Hill, N.C.: University of North Carolina Press.

RUTTER, M.
1966 *Children of Sick Parents: An Environmental and Psychiatric Study.* New York: Oxford University Press, Inc.

SCHACHTER, S.
1967 "Cognitive effects on bodily functioning: studies of obesity and overeating," in D. Glass and C. Phaffman (eds.), *Biology and Behavior: Neurophysiology and Emotion,* pp. 117–44. New York: Rockefeller University Press and Russell Sage Foundation.

————, AND J. SINGER
1962 "Cognitive, social and physiological determinants of emotional state." *Psychological Review* 69 (September):379–99.

SCHEFF, T.
1963 "Legitimate, transitional, and illegitimate mental patients in a midwestern state." *American Journal of Psychiatry* 120 (September):267–69.

———
1964a "The societal reaction to deviance." *Social Problems* 11 (Spring):401–13.

———
1964b "Social conditions for rationality: how urban and rural courts deal with the mentally ill." *American Behavioral Scientist* 8 (March):21–24.

———
1966a *Being Mentally Ill: A Sociological Theory.* Chicago: Aldine Publishing Co.

———
1966b "Users and non-users of a student psychiatric clinic." *Journal of Health and Human Behavior* 7 (Fall):114–21.

SHEARER, M., *et al.*
1968 "Unexpected effects of an 'open door' policy on birth rates of

women in state hospitals." *American Journal of Orthopsychiatry* 38 (April):413–17.

SHEPHERD, M.
1966 "Childhood behavior disorders and the child guidance clinic: an epidemiological study." *Journal of Child Psychology and Psychiatry* 7 (June):39–52.

———, *et al.*
1966 *Psychiatric Illness in General Practice.* London: Oxford University Press.

SIMMONDS, J. A.
1967 "An examination of procedures for commitment to a mental hospital." *Newsletter of the Wisconsin Psychiatric Institute,* University of Wisconsin (Fall issue):11–14.

SKINNER, B.
1962 *Walden Two.* New York: The Macmillan Company.

SKOLNICK, J. H.
1966 *Justice Without Trial.* New York: John Wiley & Sons, Inc.

SROLE, L., *et al.*
1962 *Mental Health in the Metropolis: The Midtown Manhattan Study.* New York: McGraw-Hill Book Company.

STANTON, A. H., AND M. S. SCHWARTZ
1954 *The Mental Hospital.* New York: Basic Books, Inc., Publishers.

SULLIVAN, H. S.
1953 *The Interpersonal Theory of Psychiatry.* New York: W. W. Norton & Company, Inc.

SUSSER, M.
1968 *Community Psychiatry: Epidemiologic and Social Themes.* New York: Random House, Inc.

SZASZ, T.
1960 "The myth of mental illness." *American Psychologist* 15 (February):113–18.

———
1961 *Constitutional Rights of the Mentally Ill,* Hearings before the Subcommittee of the Committee on the Judiciary, U.S. Senate. Washington, D.C.: Government Printing Office, pp. 251–72.

———
1962a "Bootlegging humanistic values through psychiatry." *Antioch Review* 22 (Fall):341–49.

1962b "Mind tapping: psychiatric subversion of constitutional rights." *American Journal of Psychiatry* 119 (October):323–27.

1963 *Law, Liberty and Psychiatry.* New York: The Macmillan Company.

1965a *Psychiatric Justice.* New York: The Macmillan Company.

1965b *The Ethics of Psychoanalysis.* New York: Basic Books, Inc., Publishers.

———, AND R. NEMIROFF
1963 "A questionnaire study of psychoanalytic practices and opinions." *Journal of Nervous and Mental Disease* 137 (September):209–21.

TAYLOR, F. K.
1966 *Psychopathology: Its Causes and Symptoms.* Washington, D.C.: Butterworths.

ULLMANN, L. P.
1967 *Institution and Outcome: A Comparative Study of Psychiatric Hospitals.* New York: Pergamon Press, Inc.

UMBARGER, C. C., *et al.*
1962 *College Students in a Mental Hospital.* New York: Grune & Stratton, Inc.

U.S. NATIONAL CENTER FOR HEALTH STATISTICS
1965 *Characteristics of Patients in Mental Hospitals—United States,* April-June, 1963.

U.S. PUBLIC HEALTH SERVICE
1965 "Survey of mental health establishments." *Mental Health Manpower* 8 (October).

1966 "Occupational and personal characteristics of psychiatrists in the United States—1965." *Mental Health Manpower* 9 (February).

WILKINS, J.
1967 "The locus of anomie in suicide." Paper presented at the 62nd Annual Meeting of the American Sociological Association.

WILSON, A. T., *et al.*
1952 "Transitional communities and social reconnection," in G.

Swanson *et al.* (eds.), *Readings in Social Psychology*, pp. 561–79. New York: Holt, Rinehart & Winston, Inc.

WING, J.
1962   "Institutionalism in mental hospitals." *British Journal of Social and Clinical Psychology* 1 (February):38–51.

———
1963   "Rehabilitation of psychiatric patients." *British Journal of Psychiatry* 109 (September):635–41.

———
1967   "The modern management of schizophrenia," in H. Freeman and J. Farndale (eds.), *New Aspects of the Mental Health Services,* pp. 3–28. New York: Pergamon Press, Inc.

———, AND G. BROWN
1961   "Social treatment of chronic schizophrenia: a comprehensive survey of three mental hospitals." *British Journal of Psychiatry* 107 (September):847–61.

WING, J., *et al.*
1967   "Reliability of a procedure for measuring and classifying 'present psychiatric state.'" *British Journal of Psychiatry* 113 (May):499–515.

WING, L., *et al.*
1967   "The use of psychiatric services in three urban areas: an international study." *Social Psychiatry* 2 (November):158–67.

WOLPE, J.
1958   *Psychotherapy by Reciprocal Inhibition.* Stanford, Calif.: Stanford University Press.

———
1966   "The conditioning and deconditioning of neurotic anxiety," in C. Spielberger (ed.), *Anxiety and Behavior,* pp. 179–90. New York: Academic Press, Inc.

YARROW, M. R.
1955   "The psychological meaning of mental illness in the family." *Journal of Social Issues* 11 (No. 4):12–24.

ZOLA, I.
1964   "Illness behavior of the working class," in A. Shostak and W. Gomberg (eds.), *Blue-Collar World: Studies of the American Worker,* pp. 351–61. Englewood Cliffs, N.J.: Prentice-Hall, Inc.

ZUSMAN, J.
1966   "Some explanations of the changing appearance of psychotic patients." *Milbank Memorial Fund Quarterly* 44 (January):363–94.

INDEX